# When Seattle *Was* . . .

How the Queen City got its kicks before emeralds,
Windows and cinnamon dolce lattes

(Volume I)

Rolin Miller and Michael Barrett

Damnation Peak Press

ISBN: 978-0-692-01701-2

Library of Congress Control Number: 2012934032

Cover and interior design by Jim Engelhardt
thehardt@wavecable.com

Cover photos by Werner Lenggenhager and Michael Barrett

Printed in the United States of America by Village Books, Bellingham, Washington

Sales and sales information available at:
— Damnation Peak Press, P.O. Box 279, Bow, WA 98232-8543
— villagebooks.com
— https://sites.google.com/site/damnationpeakpress/home
— facebook.com/damnationpeak/info

First printing May 2012
Second printing December 2012

Set in Calisto MT with Palatino Bold Titles

For our fathers, Harry and Eldon,
who knew every square foot of the Queen City
and regaled us with many
of its piquant stories.

# TABLE OF CONTENTS

BACKWARD.................................................................vii

THE JD FOLLIES...........................................................1

A MIDNIGHT CALL ON KOL...............................15

SCREENS....................................................................31

SCARING THE CRAP OUT OF ROBERT A. HEINLEIN.......47

ANOTHER DAY AT THE RACES.........................65

*THE* SPORTING LIFE................................................79

ENCOUNTER WITH A MAVERICK....................109

DIAL TONES.............................................................113

ROCKIN' RELIGION AND BROTHER RALPH...................117

THE JUMP................................................................123

TASTING THE DIFFERENCE AT DICK'S...........137

HAIL! HAIL! ROCK 'N' ROLL!..........................143

THE $10,000 FOOTBALL.....................................149

ACKNOWLEDGEMENTS....................................177

# BACKWARD

The authors came of age, or as close to it as they ever got, during the early Sixties. As pre- and early teeners, we attended different public schools in different Seattle neighborhoods that, while professing to be distinct entities, were linked by common ethnicity and the prevailing middle-class values of the day. Our paths crossed at Roosevelt High School from which we graduated in 1962, a milestone that bestowed on us a small measure of adulthood (becoming "eligible" for the military draft was perhaps the most memorable consequence of the process).

Coincidentally, the World's Fair came to town in 1962, the watershed year that many a local mover and shaker viewed as the ingredient necessary to propel the unpretentious seaport into long-suppressed adulthood (the Space Needle appears to have been the most enduring physical consequence of that process). A short time later, Seattle found itself harnessed to mainstream America by the time-shaving, four-lane interstate freeway system. With that, the town began to evolve in ways the most radical visionary probably could not have foreseen. What came to be, over the ensuing decades, was no longer the Queen City of our fathers, nor that of our own recently bygone youth. We had grown up together, the three of us, then eventually apart, as kids will when they sprout wings and fly off to chase dissimilar dreams.

What sticks out most to us, in the years between World War II and the fair, was Seattle's uniqueness. Prior to becoming the gridlocked media event dubbed the Emerald City, Puget Sound's center of commerce was an understated dot on the vast map of North America. Apart from infrequent peeks at Seattle in moviehouse newsreels—the 1919 General Strike, Boeing's Rosie the Riveter morale-boosting snapshots, the Ravenna cave-in—the town, throughout its first century, enjoyed anonymity that encouraged economic independence and development of a novel community identity bred of splendid isolation. Until the Sixties, it was a hell of a long way to the Queen City for the average motorist, travel by car being the mode of transportation preferred by an increasingly mobile American public. True, the nation craved the region's abundant salmon and timber (and, later, a growing number of 707 jetliners) and relied on the busy port for convenient access to the Far East. Otherwise, there seemed to be little reason for outsiders to venture to the geographically remote community, which had become the best-kept secret in the American West, if not the entire country. Seattle, thus, had the rare opportunity to invent itself on its own terms.

The authors grew up basking in Seattle's improvised handiwork and subsequently moved on during the years that its identity began to change. But it was not without many an affectionate look back on what the town had been—what it once was. Return with us now, if not to the stirring days of yesteryear, then to an era when Ivar Haglund was the Queen City's host and curator; Emmett Watson its crusty cultural sergeant at arms; Dorothy Bullitt its media maven; Charles Herring the town crier; Dave Beck its enforcer; Stan Boreson and J.P. Patches Seattle's court jesters; No-Mo the dog and Crazy Donkey co-mascots; Slo-Mo-Shun IV its flagship; and, in that other time, when Bill Muncey and Jim Owens approached the status of deities. Most of all, it is a visit to a place, lost in all but memory, where community goals weren't ordinarily guided by notions of *more*, *bigger* and *how much*.

This is how we knew Seattle before it got wired.

Rolin Miller and Michael Barrett

# WHEN SEATTLE *WAS* . . .

# THE JD FOLLIES

The days of spending leisurely after-school hours with *The Mickey Mouse Club* and *Wild Bill Hickok* were long gone.

It was the time of *The Blackboard Jungle* now, of rebels with and without causes. Bill Haley, America's new pop music messiah, was sucking up two out of every five nickels dropped in jukeboxes blaring his Fifties' teen anthem, "Rock Around the Clock."* DAs and waterfalls proliferated as boys' hair grew long and greasy; fingernails, too, blackened by tinkering with flathead V8s hopped up on high test. Dungarees were worn lower and lower—thin belts inserted inside waistbands to end-run Seattle Public Schools dress codes—and the dreaded black-leather jacket insinuated a cached arsenal of switchblade knives and crude, single-shot zip guns.

In the middle of it all, the summer of 1957 ended and the eighth grade began for Leonard and Roger at Nathan Eckstein Junior High.

Certain aspects of the school on Northeast Seventy-fifth didn't mesh with the jelling persona of the low-key port city. It was one of the first public institutions in town to be named for a Jew (Mr. Eckstein, who died in 1945, had been a prominent Seattle businessman and school board wheel during the Teens). But only a small number of eyebrows could have been raised by the fact because, by the time the namesake opened in 1950, hardly anyone knew who he was, let alone his religious affiliation. In fact, during the early years of the facility, Big Band-era singer Billy Eckstine was still a familiar name to a lot of undiscerning parents who supposed aloud to their equally lumpish children that Billy and Nathan were related; that somehow the brother, cousin, uncle—whatever—deserved to have a school

---

*Elvis would soon be zeroing in on the remaining three coins.

designated for him. Heck, the names *sounded* the same.[*]

By virtue of the school's appearance alone, Eckstein had an off-putting aura about it. The stark, glass-laden brick structure straddled one of the ridges wrinkling the otherwise placid face of north Seattle. Without significant surrounding landscaping to divert the eye, it stuck out against any sky like the proverbial sore thumb. When viewed from the west, especially, the school exuded the charm of a neo-California-style penal colony. The unflattering comparison may have helped cultivate the antisocial student culture that began percolating in its hallways as the Fifties bubbled along. Soon, it would become apparent that Eckstein had grown into a contradiction to the north end's cherished belief that bad adolescent behavior was confined to schools south of Madison Street.

Lily-white Eckstein became a police blotter anomaly that drew from the peaceable Ravenna, Bryant, Wedgwood and Maple Leaf neighborhoods. Moreover, many of its students were residents of three of the swellest enclaves Fifties' Seattle could boast: View Ridge, Laurelhurst and Windermere. By and large, the moms and dads from these affluent areas clung to the traditional values of the GOP, preached respectability, belonged to the PTA and nimbly juggled payments on the family's Imperial with Washington Athletic Club dues. Eckstein inherited what one might have expected to be their like-minded progeny. But some of the incoming offspring failed to share their parents' righteous regard for socioeconomic standing and proper dining-table etiquette. In fact, the school's seventh- through ninth-grade student body included an alarmingly high percentage of baby-faced thugs, sociopaths, arsonists and aspiring career criminals. Alone or in groups, they terrorized not only Eckstein, but surrounding parks, bowling alleys, movie theatres and roller rinks (this latter haunt perhaps explaining the tag "rink" that kids of the day hung on the high-profile hoods among them).

Seattle police were at first slow to deal with the elusive north-

---

[*] Never mind that Eckstein had been white, while the very visible Eckstine was black. In truth, Billy had begun life as Eckstein. Early in his career, however, a mentoring nightclub owner urged him to change the second syllable of his name to *–stine* because *–stein* was "too Jewish." The balladeer, sometimes bebopper, followed his advice.

end Dukes or the mounting evidence of rudimentary gang shenanigans. Outside of allegedly tong-infested Chinatown, such activity had virtually no precedent in Seattle's colorful history of crime and evildoing. Accordingly, perhaps, citizen complaints about increasing juvenile crime—especially car prowls and shoplifting—initially seemed to stimulate little interest at headquarters. That began to change when the howl went up from a by-God-real-life city department charging vandalism and assault in the northeast quadrant.

During the 1957-58 school year, a Seattle Transit bus assigned to haul Eckstein students home to the Greater Sand Point area was scorched inside after an impromptu bonfire was touched off using textbooks and jettisoned notebook paper. Within weeks, an eastbound driver was overpowered and thrown off his green-and-white diesel, and the bus commandeered for a joyride through the Laurelhurst neighborhood by a cadre of belligerent teens. No arrests were made in spite of there being numerous tight-lipped onlookers on board who hadn't participated in the hijacking. Seattle Transit yelled bloody murder and threatened to suspend service to the hilltop penitentiary look-and-act-alike.

The SPD sat up and took notice.

The lads had arrived at the infamous junior high as twelve-year-old strangers in September 1956 ... not by bus, but by bike. Roger hailed from an obscure elementary school on the fringes of Eckstein's territory. Leonard traded in a short-lived parochial education for the trip to public purgatory. ("They kept telling me God made it rain," he told his new chum of the decision to jump academic ships.)

Both of them showed up at the juvy jungle friendless and largely clueless. Their bonding commenced the minute they hunkered down at the very rear of their first homeroom—Mrs. Mack's brain-numbing and despotically ruled language-arts class. Yet it was soon evident that her iron hand (which Leonard grew to know all too well) was so much duck eider compared to the hazing—beatings, extortion, spit-firing squads—liberally dealt out between classes by a dedicated coalition of JDs bearing handles like "Moze," "Weebee" and "Boogie."

The neophytes, soon permanent locker partners, endured the ongoing ordeal by quickly embracing the first rule of survival at Eckstein: To rat is to die. Every day was an exercise in completely dissociating oneself from the freely dispensed floggings, trashings, (before-wedgies) pantsings, sexual harassment, muggings and threatened disembowelments (though there were few verified "stickings" on school grounds). All traces of the carnage were instantly rendered invisible even by the prey who dared not breathe a word of their victimizing to such as the Frankensteinian vice principal. And certainly not to their parents.

Over the summer, Roger nursed seventh-grade shell shock by mowing lawns and devouring the uplifting works of H.P. Lovecraft. Leonard, on the other hand, had come away from the war zone initiation energized and ready to carve his own niche at Eckstein during the coming school year. A child of the Union Bay projects, via Army posts and the lean-mean streets of Tacoma, he had perceived an opportunity to supply accoutrements as indispensable to every aspiring hoodlum as the Wildroot Cream Oil needed to pouf their pompadours. He made arrangements with the cash-deprived dropouts on his turf to fence stolen tobacco products and accessories, passing them along to the cash-heavy JDs farther north with handling fees built in. The scheme seemed to hold promise of becoming a classic win-win-win situation. Leonard could foresee no obstacles to his plan to quickly garner an eager clientele that, supplied with easily available contraband, could then concentrate on more ambitious forms of felony instead of frittering away precious misanthropic energies filching smokes from nicotine-addicted parents.

Leonard put every cent he made harvesting cascara over the summer into the fledgling enterprise. As September neared, he would take a Saturday-morning bus to wide-open First Avenue to expand his inventory by shopping the pawnbrokers located along the venerable Skid Road. He displayed a remarkable ability to haggle bargain prices for no-nos such as imported switchblades, or the kind of merchandise that saw the light of day only after a show of cash and such pre-computer passwords as "Louie sent me." Deals were closed with a wink; sales were final; receipts nonexistent.

\* \* \*

Roger missed the opening bell of Round Eight. The thought of returning to Eckstein had kept him on, or very near, the family toilet all of the first day. Edgy bowels miraculously healed by twenty-four hours of fasting, his mother wrote a sincere, if misled, excuse blaming stomach flu for Roger's absence. A pep-talking father dropped off his queasy son near the school's front door on (then *East*) Seventy-fifth before continuing to work in the company Plymouth. It was a half hour until classes convened on a lovely September morning that Roger totally failed to notice. Sighing, he entered the building and, from there, the day—the year—began its precipitous descent into Hell.

The rookie eighth-grader temporarily avoided the principal's office in hopes of locating Leonard first to get the real scoop on things before hearing the party line from a new homeroom handler. But his friend, whom he hadn't seen in nearly a week, was nowhere to be found in the uncharacteristically quiet, early-morning hallways. Roger made the decision to wait him out at their locker in spite of it fronting on a corridor wide enough to allow four future public enemies to walk abreast with the impunity of Frank Miller's gang in *High Noon.*

The first of two nasty surprises struck when the finicky combination lock finally clicked and allowed a look inside Old Number Whatever (the identifying tag, rivets and all, had long since disappeared). Roger blinked stupefaction at the assortment of goods inside that could have doubled for the contents of Sergeant Bilko's private pantry. He closed the door and quickly scanned the olive-drab exterior. A kneecap-sized dent at crotch level left no doubt about whose locker it was. He peeked again, then threw open the door wide enough to hurriedly inventory the one-by-one-by-five-foot-tall cache of merchandise crammed within: Carton after carton of Camel and Lucky Strike straights, boxes of cigars, counter display cards holding Ronson lighter fluid and flints, little gift boxes containing new and barely used Zippos, an eye-popping assortment of wicked-looking cutlery—all of it crowned by almost a dozen Whitman's Samplers. A second ogling revealed only a meager air pocket at the very top; enough room, he guessed, for one sack lunch, a single textbook and just possibly two empty Pee-Chees.

By mid-century, Seattle's downtown core was hemmed in on all sides by tacky patches: unrehabilitated Belltown to the north; the rundown upper reaches of Pike, Pine and Howell to the east; the seedy Pioneer Square district on its southern flank. But none was so wonderfully draggle-tailed as unrepentant 1st Avenue where broads, fortified wine and no-questions-asked hockshops accounted for a good share of the area's daily commerce. (Werner Lenggenhager photo courtesy of the Seattle Public Library)

Roger adjusted his slack jaw. He was trying to decide where to hide when a lightning-fast hand clapped the left shoulder of his windbreaker and sent him ceilingward. An audacious grin and a familiar voice greeted him when he landed.

"Don't worry, it'll all be gone by the time lunch is over," Leonard was there to assure him. "And, hey, welcome back."

Roger's lips twitched, but all there was of Leonard went out of focus before words could form. For Leonard, he saw, was not alone. The tall, malevolent-looking one named Weebee loomed half a foot above his friend's perky crewcut, black eyes fixed on the door of their locker like those of an attentive mamba. Roger shrank to one side as sesame opened.

Leonard extracted two cartons of Camels from the stash, dropped them in a wrinkled paper bag and passed the parcel off to Weebee as deftly as any skilled grocery clerk could have. Nothing else was exchanged. The lanky menace turned away and commenced the rink shuffle—a gait peculiar to JDs that involved widely splayed feet and a conspicuous, ape-like rolling of the shoulders—down the hall to his own locker.

To Roger's horror, Weebee failed to go the distance. A dim bulb had sparked somewhere in the darkness under the butch-waxed flattop, and the high-ranking hood reversed course. He got close enough to whisper something in his supplier's ear, a mumbling Roger wasn't able to hear. Leonard beamed enthusiastically, plucked out one of the boxes of chocolates, and placed it on an extended palm as big as a telephone book. A grudging smile flickered across Weebee's death-mask face before he turned for home base to stow the goods. "See you in class," Leonard called after him.

"You're in class with that guy?" Roger got around a second tasting of that morning's oatmeal to ask.

"So are you," Leonard replied as he rearranged his stock to accommodate Roger's belongings. "In homeroom. You and me together again. In metal shop this time. With Weebs and Seal and all those cats. And guess what?"

Roger wasn't up to speculating about anything now.

"Mister Swan made me foreman yesterday—probably because he didn't kick me out of mechanical drawing all of last year. *Foreman*, dig?" Leonard crammed Roger's new jacket in behind his lunch sack and stood back to admire the feat. "Feature me telling Stick, or Seal, or Moze to snuff a cig. Like the Crickets say, man, 'That'll be the day.'" Leonard smiled inwardly at the possibilities that lay ahead. "I tell you true, Pard, it's gonna be a crazy class. *Cra-zee*."

Roger barely realized he had handed his excuse to a chary-looking woman in the office as they passed. He stopped to gulp water and steady jellied knees at every drinking fountain on their way to the shop wing. Leonard kept up a non-stop commentary the entire distance, pausing only as he peeked through the glass insert in the door to the mandatory girl's Home Ec* class, the future homemakers' reserve. He continued after the short break. "Weebs owes me six bucks for that stuff ... going like hotcakes, man ... don't know if I can keep up with the orders coming in ... Did you get a look at the

---

* Or "ecch" to *Mad* readers of the day.

apples in Penny's sweater back there? I bet she's wearing falsies this year ... Mister Swan asked about you yesterday. Maybe you were his first choice for foreman. Too bad you were sick. Say, you still don't look too hot, man."

Leonard delivered his diagnosis as they passed the boys' gym and came to the cutoff leading east to the shop classes. Roger's face was the color of the scarred beige walls when they made the turn. He gaped down the hallway yawning before them like a dread-numbed death-row inmate facing up to the fact that his last walk would take him only as far as San Quentin's gas chamber.

The sensation was, to some extent, prophetic.

In the 1950s, Seattle's boys were condemned—*no* exceptions—to spending five of their six semesters of the junior high experience in shop classes. At Eckstein, there were four variations on the basic theme: mechanical drawing (fundamental drafting), along with wood, metal and craft shops (the latter geared to generating carloads of tacky plastic and leather doo-dads). Being subjected to the full line, it was believed, would cultivate God-fearing breadwinners—*men*—who would devote every non-wage-earning hour to activities enriched by the use of awls, T-squares, bastard files and ball-peen hammers.

Mechanical drawing was by far the most popular of the four. And for good reason. Bleeders and pacifists overwhelmingly chose it in the belief that the most serious in-class traumas inflicted by the homicidally inclined, using school property, would be limited to minor puncture wounds produced by drafting compasses. At the other extreme, metal shop drew Eckstein's juvy set like a giant junkyard electromagnet. The class offered ground-floor training for blue-collar careers both on and off McNeil Island. It also facilitated the clandestine manufacture of tools highly useful in the criminal trades: jimmies, zip guns, lockpicks, knives and the like. Metal shop also bailed out many a failing JD academician with a timely "A" or "B" mark assuring "graduation" from the eighth grade, a pivotal point at which mid-century youngsters commonly left public school in favor of a place in the voracious Fifties' job market.

For the well-connected Weebees of that world, however, metal shop was both a recreational and educational experience—an unequaled opportunity to scheme, gear up, reconnoiter and utterly terrorize the weak and fearful in a captive classroom environment.

Shop classes were confined to an isolated wing of the school. A battle-savvy architect had designed Eckstein with an eye to limiting damage from explosions and sudden conflagrations to the annex itself. Big, combat-seasoned men like six-and-a-half-foot-tall Mr. Swan ruled their unruly roosts like POW camp commandants aided by effective enforcement ordnance. Juggling mechanical drawing and metal shop duties, he armed himself with the legendary Mr. Goodyear, an old, treadless sneaker that, after spanking an offender's open palm at warp speed, rendered the dominant hand useless and, hence, harmless for up to an hour. Mr. Goodyear snuffed out malfeasance instantly, broke up many a fight, and even intervened in at least one life-or-death situation. The year before, a wake-up blow to the head of a Wedgwood-bred kamikaze interrupted the boy's attempt to cut through the side of a fifty-pound bottle of acetylene with a welding torch. Had the lad's efforts succeeded, the resulting blast would have registered on seismographs in San Diego.

Across the hall, Mr. Wiggins maintained a modicum of peace in craft shop with a sawed-off cricket bat that delivered abasing "swats" to various body parts. The school board, Eckstein staff and most parents applauded the liberal use of corporal punishment as a way of keeping the cell-block population in line and the building intact. Fits of conscience attributable to the practice were unknown.

In spite of its numerous and varied hazards, metal shop had its passionate devotees. Hide (or was it Hyde?) and LaFranz, Eckstein's titans of truancy, seldom missed class, barring occasional police interviews. The pair spent the entire semester secretly working—with brass, tin, then copper—on trying to mass-produce counterfeit quarters and half dollars usable in the booming economy's widening array of vending machines.

Boogie, on the other hand, obsessed over the shop's metal bender. The spring-driven apparatus, capable of shaping anything lighter than plate steel, required considerable strength to operate. Once the metal piece had been crooked to specifications, the fabricator faced the daunting task of slowly relaxing a powerful jaw capable of crushing a Renault Dauphine, if abruptly released. Early on, Boogie began getting ghoulish kicks by allowing the heavy-duty bender to slam back into its open position. The sound achieved was akin to the impact of colliding freight trains and, within the enclosed shop space, rattled both window glass and perpetually frayed nerves. Boogie's astonishing lateral jumping ability, which would have earned him gold had it been a sanctioned Olympics event, propelled him to his workbench a split second before the thunderous *boom*. Invariably, an innocent bystander nearest the machine garnered Mr. Goodyear's blind wrath for causing the disturbance. Boogie and his bender were to be closely watched every minute.

Seal toiled for weeks making a delicate copper leaf-and-wire candleholder for his hopelessly alcoholic mother. It had nearly been completed when, in early November, incidental roughhousing during lunch caused him to go berserk à la Jimmy Cagney in *White Heat*. The combined efforts of three male teachers and two janitors were required to bulldog the unhinged teen out of the packed lunchroom. Seal was one of the first to permanently disappear from the eighth-grade lineup. Leonard found his project at the bottom of the shop's scrap bucket as he tidied up before the Christmas break. The abandoned candleholder had been tightly wound around the shaft of a long screwdriver and reduced to dreck in one of the big vises.

Three years later, at sixteen, Seal lost his life in a hayriding accident outside of Stanwood, north of Seattle.

Roger, on the other hand, died a little each weekday. From the moment he trudged past the scent of Babbo or a Duncan Hines creation being whipped up in Home Ecch, and turned down the smoggy, burnt-smelling corridor leading to the shops, his belly seemed to fill with just-poured cement. First thing each morning, homeroom confronted him with the resurrected horrors of Dante's *Inferno* and the Battle of Gettysburg, with the London Blitz thrown in to foster still more excruciating anxiety. Metal shop was a veritable mine field of booby traps that ranged from slow-fused small explosives to fresh rubber cement hurriedly smeared on workbench surfaces, which doubled as seating during compulsory roll call. Even the ruling JD faction had to exercise care before alighting on most level spots in the room. For until combat-ready Zippos were employed to burn off fabric-eating adhesives, the unwary stood a good chance of contracting the dreaded "sticky ass" for the remainder of the school day (which, on the bright side, usually exempted the afflicted from pantsings).

Mr. Swan possessed a remarkable eyes-in-the-back-of-the-head cognition that bordered on clairvoyance. His knack for sniffing out imminent disaster was, however, limited to time actually spent at the ongoing crime scene. Some laid his frequent absences to serious nic fits. Others had heard tell that speculating on stocks drove him to make impulsive transactions over an outside phone line available in the heavily fortified teachers' lounge. Whatever the reason, Mr. Swan would periodically duck out of class and leave the danger-laden anthill in the hands of his student foreman.

Leonard shared Mr. Swan's instinct for smelling catastrophe in the making, but seldom did anything to prevent it unless his own life was imperiled. Given the certainty of retribution for squealing, there was simply no percentage in doing otherwise. Leonard was, however, sympathetic to the plight of his less-street-smart friend, and repeatedly updated Roger on the odds of there being a mob-planted cherry bomb (or his own) about to go off in the coal-fed forge. In addition, his keen nose was always one of the first to detect natural gas escaping from one or more of the small annealing ovens near the rear of the big room. The unmistakable rotten-egg smell usually provided a ten-second or so window in which to take cover with Roger before Moze aimed and fired his clothespin match gun at the growing cloud of invisible fumes. Those who came away from the initiation by firebomb with singed arm hair quickly learned that Moze was yet another classmate to be carefully monitored.

More than once, Roger's improving radar enabled him to return the favors. One morning, he looked up from misshaping a length of wrought iron to spot a flaming four-foot-long missile fashioned from kraft paper bearing down on the back of Leonard's head. With a move that rivaled the best of Boogie's, he leapt the width of two workstations to body-block his friend out of its path. The mini-Hindenburg reenacted its infamous Lakehurst, New Jersey, landing in a remote corner beyond the disabled lathing machines.

The incident said all there was to say about two sets of vigilant eyes being better than one in this, the original shop of horrors.

In spite of his elevated status as purveyor to Eckstein's criminal set, Leonard faced bankruptcy within sixty days of start-up. The locker he shared with Roger was devoid of goods by then. But his pockets were empty as well. Leonard had settled for too many verbal promises of payment, along with a fistful of illegible IOUs. Soon, he owed overdue cash to his sources that he simply didn't have. He had been slow to react to the trend and face the fact that the bulk of his clientele were both bullies and deadbeats from whom five-nine, 125-pound Leonard stood a snowball's chance of collecting pocket lint. To make matters worse, the ranks of the four-flushers began thinning as the semester ground on.

Faced with a financial bath, and finding himself threatened by impatient suppliers, Leonard modified his benign approach to dealing with the indebted he was carrying on his books. Experience had taught him to avoid direct confrontations with the blatantly sociopathic among his clientele. His only face-off over money owing had found him unconscious in front of his locker after a run-in with a tough known from then on as The Strangler.

Leonard began to broaden his role as shop foreman to include tactics that would have done a seasoned skip tracer proud. Misfortune began befalling legitimate class projects belonging to the slow-to-pay. The forge, which Leonard was responsible for tending, commenced behaving badly. In spite of solemn claims he was going by the book, his furious cranking of its bellows could whip the thing into simulating Mt. Vesuvius at its most tempestuous. Spewing white-hot cinders from its bowels, the angry forge was capable of reducing a chiseler's chisel stock to an unrecognizable lump. Select projects disappeared before they could be graded. Inconspicuous flaws in even the most painstaking work failed to escape Leonard's critical eye and, in confidential powwows, were brought to Mr. Swan's less-exacting attention.

Freeloaders in danger of flunking the eighth grade inched toward the downhill side of D-bound-for-E country (F was not on the accepted grading scale then). During the final weeks of Leonard's regime, the recalcitrant found cinch A's eroding away to B's, even

C-pluses, unless old bills were settled and accounts squared. When the cash came through, the forge grew tame again; the foreman's critiques became less fussy; missing projects miraculously reappeared from overlooked cubbyholes.

The tide turned for Leonard—but in the wrong direction for Mr. Swan's rogues' gallery. A few of the nimbler minds over at the Wallingford Precinct began to ID Eckstein as the epicenter of the north end's troubling juvenile crime wave. Key arrests fingered Mr. Swan's now-infamous homeroom as especially fertile ground for police investigations. Ultimately, the attention kicked off a series of after-school, third-degree sessions.

Every enrollee was forced to come to grips with the stigma of being traceable to Mr. Swan's notorious day-care for desperados. Hall monitors were dispatched all over the school, typically during sixth period on a Friday, to hand-deliver official summonses from the principal's office to those presumed guilty by virtue of answering "here" during morning roll call. Everyone in the class was required to return to homebase for grilling before being formally dismissed from school. The ongoing interrogation program dragnetted better-than-expected results and, as squad cars pulled away from the campus carrying each tribunal's catch, more and more open crime files could be stamped CASE CLOSED. Accordingly, fewer and fewer of the leather-jacketed element were present to sneer expletives when their names were called by Mr. Swan in the weeks that followed.

Leonard and Roger were normally eliminated from the list of usual suspects within an hour. The foreman was never linked to the projects' gang, nor clearly identified as a fence. Roger's transgressions—stuffing spuds up a Kaiser Manhattan's tailpipe and gracing the porches of cranky neighbors with flaming bags of doody—weren't yet punishable by doing time at Green Hill Reformatory.

Leonard convinced Mr. Swan that his duties as second in command rated a top mark. Mission accomplished, he then lobbied to land his battle-fatigued friend a kind of honorary "A" for being an aboveboard kid and upstanding citizen. The grade certainly wasn't to be based on output. Roger had completed only one project during the entire term, a wobbling, three-legged bar stool crowned by a foam-rubber seat wrapped in Naugahyde—an instant black-and-chartreuse white elephant. Mr. Swan caved in to his foreman's salesmanship and went on to show mercy to the rest of the traumatized by handing out nothing lower than a "B" (presumably to reward their survival skills).

The friends marked the end of the ordeal by attending a Saturday matinee featuring *Attack of the 50-Ft. Woman.* The movie was a colossal bust, as hoped, giving generous exposure to Allison Hayes' fifty-foot bosom. The following week they were randomly assigned to new shop adventures—Leonard to wood second period and Roger to Mr. Wiggins' far-calmer craft conclave in the afternoon. They shared no classes that last semester of the eighth grade, but commuted to school and lunched together every day while constantly touching bases at their now-tidy locker.

Meanwhile, after clearing the Albertson's parking lot west of Roosevelt Way in another part of town, two other locker partners paused while the shorter of the pair lit a Lucky Strike from a pack fresh out of a vending machine at the nearby bowling alley. He blew the smoke upwind, away from his friend, and tracked the course they had taken along Ravenna Boulevard from John Marshall Junior High School.

"What are you doing tomorrow?" Jules asked the skinny lad who sported thick glasses and a pronounced Adam's apple.

"Gee, I don't know yet," Mike replied over the roar of a lowered '51 Chev bound for Green Lake. "What are you doing?"

Jules scratched his precocious five-o'clock shadow before taking another deep drag. "I'm going to jump on an early bus headed for First Avenue."

"Neato."

"The thing is, the pawn shops down there give really good buys right after they open on Saturday—cool stuff guys like Dave would pay a lot to get their hands on. Why don't you come along for a look?"

Seattle was very different then. But the blend of long-lost ingredients made for lifelong friends.

# A MIDNIGHT CALL ON KOL

In unison, they tossed their empties into the blackberry-choked ravine below West Massachusetts Street.

It was a half hour before midnight, time to desert the stunning view of downtown Seattle for their beds in the north end. Leonard and Roger usually made a lukewarm effort to abide by nominal 12:30 A.M. curfews. Danny the Driver, a Roosevelt senior, had to get home, too. He faced compulsory family duties most of Easter day and took his father's big right hand very seriously when considering the consequences of truancy. (Jules, the firstborn of Old Country parents, had been able to name his own hours from the moment he earned his driver's license at sixteen. The trouble was, Jules wasn't piloting his folks' VW bus that night.) On top of the foregoing constraints, the evening's second case of Olympia hauled from the trunk an hour before had grown warm and, when warm, ranked right up there with Vano liquid when it came to palatability.

A moment later, Danny turned right on Ferry and started along the pocked gravel street. Jules asked him to go easy before angling onto the straightaway that drops down to Harbor Avenue. They slowly cruised the house near the corner, the place that displayed a slew of Christmas character cutouts the lads had rearranged in December. There was damned little in life that was funnier, they reckoned, than winding up a festive night in West Seattle with Rudolph's red nose pressed up against Vixen's heinie.

Tonight, on the way up Ferry to their hallowed drinking grounds, the merrymakers had spotted two big Easter bunnies and a giant plywood egg in the very same yard. During much of the evening of libation and uninhibited palaver, Jules had secretly planned how to creatively reconfigure the holiday exhibit. A vision inspired by the *Kama Sutra* came to him just as he cracked his seventh beer. In that instant, it became clear what Thumper and his pal would be doing to outrage the neighborhood when it arose in a few hours to attend sunrise services.

Danny immediately kiboshed the plan when it was finally let out of the bag, effectively nipping the prank in the bud by goosing the gas pedal. No way would he allow his flaky pals to track mud, rocks and dog crap into his cherry '57 Ford Fairlane. Although he had kept it to himself, he had become increasingly alarmed by how much beer his exuberant passengers were putting away. Four bottles were just about his limit. *These* guys had already downed more than twice that amount and continued to lap it up like bone-dry camels. Oh, horror of horrors if one of them barfed in the back seat.

Danny gave his black beauty more gas, hoping to G-force the clamoring bingers against the seat cushions. Jules responded to the jolt by toasting the big blue-and-white welding flashes visible from the sprawling Harbor Island industrial park below. He followed the salute by proposing they scour Alki Avenue for Latvians Maris and his brother Booby. Roger and Leonard seconded the motion. Danny reacted by turning up the radio.

There were only two AM stations worth diddly in the Seattle market, as far as Danny was concerned. Actually, only one now. Danny had recently become a KJR man and the Ford's on-board Philco expressed his devotion. Four of the radio's selector buttons were prepunched to the 950 channel. The fifth, on the far right, was locked on 1300, *way* up the dial. KOL.

KOL, until recently rock radio's Big Daddy of the local airwaves, had lost a lot of ground to its chief competitor during the past year. Manager Archie Taft and the station's ownership had unwisely elected to man KOL's mics with seasoned veterans like Ray Hutchinson, Chuck Ellsworth and Al Cummings. Collectively, they formed an outstanding pool of laid-back talent that appealed to an ever-younger demographic like a favorite high school chemistry teacher equipped with a turntable. Down the dial, however, KJR's foresighted program director, John Stone, had begun assembling a stable of boyish, silver-tongued screamers who were soon dominating the Hooper ratings in virtually every time slot. From the very early Sixties on, it paid a cool cat like Danny to be aware of Lee Perkins' best zinger of the day; to know what catchphrase Dick Curtis had planted out in radioland; to be up on Pat O'Day's sweaty hops where a teen on the make might stand a chance of getting lucky.

KOL? KOL earned one button only because Danny, high on foot-stompin' rock and down on the slow stuff, would sometimes give 1300 a quick listen during those rare times when a KJR jock would spin a little too much of The Browns, Ferrante and Teicher or, lord forbid, Lawrence "Turn on the Bubble Machine" Welk. The other R&R stations in the area—KAYO and Wally Nelskog's Cuties on its fringes—provided alternatives, too. But what image-conscious Roosevelt High stud would want to be caught listening to those second-rate AM-pop-culture pissants? Danny knew the answer, but doubted quasi-beatniks like Leonard, Roger and Jules did.

KJR's Terry Rose, the 6:00 P.M.-to-midnight guy on Saturdays, had begun skating on thin ice, in Danny's opinion, when he followed Paul Anka's sappy "Tonight My Love, Tonight" with Kathy Young's whiny "Happy Birthday Blues" (which, that week, was weighing in at Number Nine on the Fabulous Fifty Music Survey). The last barrage of empty stubbies was still tinkling down in the Massachusetts Street briar patch when Rose really hacked off Danny by playing a novelty tune called "Three Wheels on My Wagon" by some no-name nudnik named Dick Van Dyke. Danny's sense of humor was as short as a Teddy letterman's hair in those days, and his loathing for music even remotely hinting of "Country and Western" roots bordered on psychotic.

But it was eye-filling Annette who really pushed his buttons and, ultimately, the Philco's following an urgent call of nature halfway down the hill. Miss Funicello had barely dented the first verse of "Dream Boy" when Danny's guided-missile forefinger sent the dial indicator rocketing to the right. On KOL, happily, The Marcels were winding up every pop station's chart-topper, "Blue Moon," the industry's all time "bom-a-bom-bom, a-dangy-dang-dang" hit.* Danny was instantly in the groove and joined in the bring-it-all-home "bluuuuue mmmooooon" finale, with the three guzzlers lending voice to a truly distasteful *a cappella* omelette.

---

* Coast-to-coast, the song had soared to Number One faster than any platter since the Everlys' "Wake Up Little Susie" in 1957.

Six stations rocked the AM radio band from Renton to Everett in the Fifties and early Sixties: 910 KQDE (Swingin' 60), 950 KJR (Fabulous 50), 1090 KING (30 Lucky List of Hits), 1150 KAYO (Top 50/Giant 62), 1230 KQTY (Swingin' 60) and KOL (40 Top Tunes/Top 40/Sizzlin' 60/Solid 60/Project 40/Top 40 Tunedex). DJ Art Simpson, here seen clowning for a publicity photo, had the misfortune of pulling the evening shift at KOL Easter Eve of 1961. (Bill Taylor Collection)

\* \* \*

DJ Art Simpson segued with a quip about Lorenz Hart spinning in his grave every time The Marcels' version of his song was aired. Danny had no idea who Lorenz Hart was, but tensed in anticipation of what Simpson would serve next off the KOL Solid Sixty menu. Although two-thirds in the bag, Jules saw the opportunity to expand the scope of the evening's activities. "Art Simpson is right over there, by that tower," he said, leaning over the seat to yell in the Driver's ear. For good measure, Jules pointed to the endless groupings of huge arc lights illuminating the length and breadth of Seattle's maritime heart.

"What's he doing there?" Danny wanted to know as he slowed his rumbling steed to get a better look from their elevated vantage point.

"KOL's on Harbor Island," Jules explained. There was no reaction. "You know, the KOL studio—the place where Art's broadcasting from." (Simpson, at that moment, was in the middle of a scripted spiel for Hansen Baking's Sunbeam bread franchise.)

Danny allowed time for the news to work its way through a layer of anesthetized brain cells. "No kidding?" he drawled after the fact had bored in farther. "Art Simpson's right down *there*?"

Leonard was the Danny connection from school and had arranged for the senior to chauffeur that night. By the time they were set to leave West Seattle, Jules had known Danny for something just short of five hours. But that had been ample time for him to get a handle on how to screw with the automotive shop fixture. "Got any records you want to hear?" Jules asked innocently enough.

Danny responded with uncommon speed. "Dammit, we haven't heard Rockin' Robin for a long time," he complained. In reality, Terry Rose had spun the Northwest's quintessential "Louie Louie"* just after 9:00. At that exact moment, however, bursting bladders had driven all of them staggering down dead-end Victoria Avenue seeking relief. Rose was blameless for Danny's deprivation.

"I'll bet Art here would spin Rockin' Robin if we asked," Jules suggested casually. "Especially if we asked in person."

"No doubt about it," Roger slurred after blasting the back of Leonard's head with a point-blank beer belch.

So began the chant: "Loo-way. Loo-way. Loo-way."

By the time Danny had hung a right on Harbor Avenue, the Fairlane's throaty duals were mere background fipple flutes overwhelmed by the booming incantations filling the interior of the car. The only competing mayhem in the Youngstown District late that night came from a complement of workers from the nearby

---

* The gazillion seller—The Kingsmen's one-take rip-off of the Roberts-Dangel retooling of the Richard Berry classic—was still two years away.

Bethlehem Steel plant. After shift, a thirsting crew had flooded the Blew Eagle across Spokane Street and was making serious headway raising the roof off the legendary hangout's who-needs-a-jigger bar. As the lads passed on the way to Harbor Island, the Eagle's beleaguered staff was fighting every Saturday's losing battle trying to enforce Washington State's midnight booze curfew. To a steel worker with three prepaid boilermakers coming at last call, a barmaid's suggestion that they be collected on Monday would inevitably provoke a thundering "Gimme 'em NOW!"

Art Simpson was treating his audience to another lunar-themed hit, "There's a Moon Out Tonight," when he decided to give his cramping legs a stretch. He relit a trademark Roi-Tan and walked stiffly into KOL's darkened outer offices, keeping an ear peeled to be sure The Capris were coming across the intercom. To his regret, he found the group harmonizing loud and clear. The song's moronic lyrics inspired him to blow a perfect smoke ring at the half-pallet load of boxed chocolate Easter eggs shoved against the west wall. The station had not been able to give away most of the wretched things as part of a lame holiday promotion. He brushed the top of his short-cropped salt-and-pepper hair and tried not to wonder whether this week's paycheck would clear the bank.

Simpson encountered middle age while radio lay on its deathbed. In less than a decade, The Empire of the Air had shriveled to a courtyard-sized shadow of its former might. Only recently had the withering wireless industry begun to seriously reinvent itself, chiefly by appealing to specialized, local tastes. As network feeds dwindled and affiliations ended, more and more AM stations became independents desperately seeking to hang onto millions of adult listeners being sucked away by the boob tube. One dawn-to-dark license in town (KXA) devoted its programming to classical music. KGDN dedicated its airtime to God. Another, KNBX, was tinkering with a Country and Western format. And down in the Bay Area, KGO even let a guy named Ira Blue talk to callers all night. Imagine.

But in the Seattle-Everett market, youth and rock were pampered royally, and five Top-40 (-50, -60) stations to choose from on the dial said all there was to say about format radio.

Simpson chewed two Tums to keep a gallon of rancid coffee in line and glowered at the Royal Crown Cola clock glowing in one corner of the morgue-like office. 11:48. Where in hell was the new midnight-to-5:30 guy, Jerry Kay, anyway? Kay had called in about an hour earlier to warn Simpson that he might be cutting it close, and it appeared now he meant to keep his word. Simpson tugged on his bowtie and noted that The Capris were, mercifully, winding down. He was about to return to the mic when a pair of headlight beams on Florida Street raked the front of the building and lurched to a stop out front. Anticipating that his relief had once again forgotten his keys, Simpson hobbled across the room, released the lock on the entry door and hurried back the way he had come.

The veteran skillfully spliced the opening of "But I Do" into The Capris' flamboyant finale, then hunched over the nearly exhausted sponsor's schedule searching for a "commercial word" to insert after "Frogman" Henry concluded his opus. Simpson was scanning copy plugging Clark's Round the Clock when, out of the corner of his eye, he saw the studio door bump open. Before looking up, he concocted an exquisitely barbed salute to fire at the almost-tardy midnight man. The peevish greeting never got past his Adam's apple.

Maybe it had something to do with the lateness of the hour. Or perhaps it was Nature's way of telling him to wear his glasses all the time. Whatever the cause, he found that Jerry Kay had divided himself into four parts. Simpson blinked again. No, Jerry had transformed himself into four separate beings. Young beings. Teenagers. Four *scruffy*-looking teenagers. Four very unwelcome scruffy-looking teenagers blocking any hope he had of escaping the small and suddenly claustrophobic-feeling broadcast booth. Four teens with red, bleary eyes who seemed almost as stunned by the encounter as the captive DJ.

Simpson studied them critically, as he would have a bad poker hand, and slowly withdrew the Roi-Tan while his pulse leveled off. "You guys see the sign above the door?" he demanded with the civility of a junior high vice principal.

As one, the lads craned their necks in reverse and squinted up at the little box above the dusty molding under which they had just passed.

Simpson warned, "When it lights up—when it says ON THE AIR—it means I'm on live. And that means you zip it up or else all seventy-three people listening to me will hear you guys over the air. Got it?"

A lot of ardent chin-wagging indicated, *yes*, they understood.

Ever the professional, Simpson pointed to the sign and—a minute late—called out the station's top-of-the-hour identification. With Connie Francis calming things down a bit, Simpson sized up the group again and failed to find any evidence of weapons or openly hostile intent. The quartet just hung together, clotting, inside the narrow doorway. The aging jock's expression soured as he studied this rare and deeply disturbing manifestation of his late-night fan base. He checked the sound level, adjusting a couple of Bakelite knobs and finally worked up the energy to ask, "So, who are you guys, anyway?"

Finding himself a half-step ahead of the others, Leonard felt compelled to speak first. He cleared his throat and tagged himself without revealing his often-mispronounced surname.

"His last name sounds like *useless*," Danny volunteered. "That's what we call him."

Simpson grudgingly nodded understanding. "Useless, hunh? Where are you from, Useless—West Seattle? Rat City?"

"The north end," Leonard told him.

"Roosevelt High," Danny rushed to elaborate.

"Roosevelt, hunh?" Simpson seemed vaguely impressed. "I didn't know anybody north of the Canal could hear us."

"Absolutely ... You bet ... Rain or shine," came a flurry of testimonials.

"So what brings you all the way down here to exotic Harbor Island?"

Danny wasn't about to mince words. "We want to hear 'Louie Louie.'"

Simpson's baggy eyes narrowed. "Then you'd better tune in Brand X."

"Brand *X*?"

"Brand X ... Payola 95 ... K-Junior—whatever it is you kids call it," Simpson blustered. "I already played The Wailers once tonight.

About forty-five minutes ago." He gave each of them and accusatory once-over. "Guess that means you weren't listening to me."

"The—*our*—radio was off," Jules stammered.

"We were walking around the beach," Leonard fibbed. Badly.

Danny turned chalk white.

"Look, I'm no Johnny Stone type. I don't have to play any goddamned house bands four times an hour. And as far as 'Louie Louie' is concerned … *cripers!*'" It wasn't clear whether Simpson's vocalized epiphany was directed at his profane slip of the tongue, or if he had suddenly become conscious of Connie's gut-wrenching bleating that signaled an end to "Where the Boys Are." What *was* clear to Danny's gang was that the smoldering cigar had been aimed at the ON THE AIR sign just as the record ended.

The mic went live. "Have you worked up a bad case of the hungries cruising around tonight?" the DJ ad-libbed for the benefit of all the bar ejectees now fanning out across the city. In pre-Denny's 1961, the hunt for post-midnight vittles presented a big challenge for the town's after-hours set; amazing, but true, given a population hovering around 550,000. If the Round the Clock or the Blew Eagle failed to fill the bill at, say, 2:15 in the morning, then precious few choices remained for the common man apart from Bob Murray's Dog House and the wonderfully wacky Hasty-Tasty up in the U-District.

Seattle's hefty contingent of bluenoses sought to portray the port city as a place where everybody went to bed at 10:30—even on weekends. According to the myth, its citizens craved only Mom's home cooking after that hour. In reality, the town's legitimate all-night eateries, scarce as they were, did a land-office business.*

Simpson was extolling the virtues of a pre-Atkins steak-links-bacon breakfast as the lads shifted positions in an effort to get comfortable in the cramped space. As they stirred, someone behind Leonard clipped the back of his right knee. Leonard, balance in jeopardy, clawed the air ahead to steady himself and swept fifty demo

---

* Numerous after-hours clubs were also in operation at the time. But hash browns and hamburger steaks weren't to be found on the menus offered by hot spots like the New Chinatown.

records off an adjacent typewriter stand. The stack of avalanching 45s slid into five years worth of *Billboard Magazine*, bringing the whole caboodle crashing down on the linoleum floor. Everybody in the room jumped. Leonard quickly regained his equilibrium, however, and received a punishing look from Simpson as a reward.

The Hasty-Tasty, 5247 University Way, in 1960. Dedicated to cholesterolemia and free-flowing black coffee, this "always open" magnet drew UofW insomniacs, rounders, lonely hearts, stoners, the Beat Generation, starving night owls and the dispossessed from all over the northend. The wee hours there were a study in the workings of a motley social anthill the SPD chose only to wink at. (Keivan Allafzadeh/Mars Bistro Collection)

"… So if you're up early tearing down a house, like we are here," the DJ glided through the unwelcome sound effect, "remember the mouth-watering possibilities awaiting every taste, right this very minute, at Clark's Round the Clock at Olive and Terry." Simpson's eyes remained glued on Leonard until the turntable's arm dropped on a soon-to-be-smash-hit called "Runaway." Out went the ON THE AIR sign.

"Sorry," Leonard peeped.

"Yeah, yeah." Simpson waved him off as he rose from his chair. "Listen, Useless. I've got a job for you and your mob. But you have to be quick." He shooed the willing herd down the hall to the office, flipped on the lights and motioned them over to the west wall. "Put your arms out straight," he barked, demonstrating the desired pose for the slow to comprehend. Four sets of hands, palms up, were obediently extended and loaded with surplus Easter eggs, compliments of the cigar-chomping provisioner.

"Gees, this's a heckuva lotta chocolate," Roger crowed to the dozen or so boxed goodies clasped to his chest.

"I want to make points up there in Lynxland," Simpson explained, without much conviction, as he hustled the encumbered foursome toward the front door.

"The Lynx are from Lincoln," Danny pointed out. "We're the Roughriders."

"Whoopty-damn-do," Leonard singsonged under his breath.

"Good for you, boys," their reluctant host congratulated them through a swirling cloud of smoke. "Just hand the things out to your buddies, family, neighbors, girlfriends—" he looked over the wobbly troupe with thinly disguised skepticism "—anyway, to your buddies, family and neighbors. Anybody with a strong stomach. And remember to mention 1300 KOL."

Over the speakers behind him, a frenzied electric organ had completed its mid-record solo and Del Shannon, for a final time, puzzled "why-why-why-why-why, she ran away." There was a green-apple-two-step urgency to Simpson's gait as he drove the Roosevelt High legation out the door.

"There won't be much of Easter left when you come to," he yelled after them, "so get on the stick. And keep your jalop between the ditches!" The aging disc jockey displayed uncommon agility shooting the deadbolt and bounding for the rear of the building.

"Gees, this's a helluva lotta eggs." Roger had no one to convince but himself after two of the boxes had fallen to the pavement, unnoticed, somewhere back in the darkness.

It required five minutes to stow the serendipitous cargo, then themselves, following a mandatory parking-lot pee call. Danny swerved slightly to avoid blinding by an oncoming pair of headlights, then guided his Ford onto the service street where he laid rubber in the direction of the Blew Eagle. A block behind Danny's taillights, Jerry Kay jumped out of his car and frowned down at four wet patches and three crushed confectionery boxes circling his parking spot outside the station. Kay reached the locked front door before realizing he had forgotten the station key back at his apartment.

Black coffee was now being dispensed by the bucketful at the Eagle. The smell of scorched hamburger, crisping potatoes and bad cholesterol poured from every kitchen vent as Danny wheeled past the throbbing noshery. Four sets of whetted ears hung on every word their newfound hero, now in Easter Day overtime, had to say about Verv Alertness Capsules ("... They combat fatigue almost immediately, and keep you alert and full of pep hour, af-ter hour, af-tah 'our'err," Simpson japed to keep himself awake). Art's replacement, on the other hand, was expending his energy stumbling around the front of the station pounding on every pane of glass he could reach.

Up the road, Leonard had begun grousing to his cohorts while he tentatively munched a slab of flavorless chocolate shell trimmed with brittle pink and yellow marzipan: "This thing tastes like shit."

Jules took the critique to the next level and spat his mouthful out the window. "Especially with beer."

"Can it!" Danny ordered them. "*Listen!*"

Art Simpson's gravelly voice reached out to them like an old friend's through the front and rear speakers. "So how are you doing out there, Midnighters?" It was as if his question was directed right at them.

A thunderous "BITCHIN', ART!" rocked the Fairlane.

"I'm in extra innings tonight," Simpson told them while, out in the dark, Jerry Kay groped his way to the back of the building. "The big news is, I just finished visiting with Leonard Useless and his useless buddies," the jock prattled on. "And Leonard, old boy, I've got a platter here I bet pretty well sums up what kind of progress you're making on the way home tonight."

The Teddy left-outs focused every ounce of attention on the immortal words that began flowing from the Philco.

*Three wheels on my wagon,*
*and I'm still rolling along...*

"Who *is* that shitkicker?" Danny bellowed loud enough to be heard in Burien. "Christ on the Cross!"

*The Cherokees are chasin'—*

Danny punched young Mr. Van Dyke into AM oblivion as the vertical red stripe zipped left on the dial at just under the speed of sound.

He had missed the opening riff (*duh duh duh, duh duh*) of "Louie Louie" on KJR by ten seconds.

Most of the valet-parked cars had been delivered, and the Broadmoor set began weaving its way home up Madison. Victor

When serious plans for a local world's fair weren't being hatched at the Washington Athletic Club, the Queen City boosters often gravitated to Victor Rosellini's mid-town watering holes. The Four 10 was forced to move from its original home in the White-Henry-Stuart Building in 1975. It finished out its days (until 1989) at the 4th Avenue and Vine location, perhaps symbolically situated in the shadow of the Space Needle championed by Victor and his well-placed clientele. (Werner Lenggenhager photo courtesy of the Seattle Public Library)

Rosellini, vice chair of the Washington State World's Fair Commission, locked the door behind them. He smiled. If any group was capable of shaking its own Beefeaters martinis from now till Easter services, it was that bunch.

Mr. R had personally closed the Four-10 tonight, and that month's lounge act quickly drifted out the back way. Vic returned to the Boulevard Room—a bar that had never seen a Roi-Tan—and took stock through a Havana-cigar-smoke haze of the local nobility crowding his watering hole. He nodded to his cousin Al, the governor, then down the line at Gordon Clinton, Seattle's mayor, and one-by-one at the likes of Eddie Carlson, Al Rochester, Paul Friedlander, Maggie, Tom Pelly and at a dozen other notables of rare like-mind gathered under one roof. Three taps with sterling ice tongs on the side of a raised tumbler silenced his guests. Following the lead of their host, a keglet of fifteen-year-old single malt, neat, was raised on high.

"Gentlemen," the engaging restaurateur began, "we are but one year and nineteen days away from our goal."

Wheels of all weights and sizes were turning in Seattle that night.

Without question, Tai Tung is the patriarch of Seattle Chinese restaurants (and on its way to becoming the longest-lasting in any culinary category). While never an all-nighter, long-time manager Harry Chan stresses that, for decades, the King Street café was open until 3:45 A.M., seven days per week … late enough that untold thousands of Seattle revelers were able to trim blood-alcohol readings with generous portions of Tai Tung's legendary chop suey. (Werner Lenggenhager photo courtesy of the Seattle Public Library)

# SCREENS

The Broadway. The Madrona. The Lake City. The Ballard. The Green Lake. The Magnolia. The Columbia. The Hi-Line. The Beacon. The Burien.... It seemed as if every Seattle neighborhood worthy of a name had one in the Fifties: a theatre. A picture show, as opposed to porno palaces and hootchy-kootch houses. Each was a well-defined entity easily distinguishable from today's multiple-screen cineplexes woven into the architectural DNA of modern shopping malls and self-contained retail beehives.

Back when, Seattle could claim only Northgate as a line item on its one-stop shopping list, a visionary template for suburban peddling to come (way out in the boonies on E. 110th). The Northgate Theatre, blueprinted on the hem of the complex from its inception, wrote the book on the expediency of including a movie venue in every mall able to attract Sears Roebuck and a Thom McAn shoe store.

Owing to its aloof, gun-emplacement styling, Sterling Theatres' Northgate was something of an anomaly in the early Fifties. But beneath its stark exterior beat the heart of a traditional one-lunger sporting only a single, albeit huge, silver screen.

Eisenhower-era movie houses helped distinguish the town's neighborhoods from one another in a day when geographical, racial and cultural distinctions mattered deeply to Seattleites. Most theatres were long-established by then, many dating back to an age before soundtracks on film. Design and architecture varied widely, ranging from downtown's opulent Paramount (originally the Seattle Theatre) to humbler showplaces like the Hollywood on pre-one-way Roosevelt Northeast. None were multiplexes and the majority, by the Fifties, were locally owned as a consequence of vigorous federal monopoly-busting of the once dominant studio-controlled chains.

The Arabian, blocks north of Green Lake on Aurora, occupied this building from 1925 until its closure in 1954. The theatre was emblematic of theme-garnished movie houses that once abounded in Seattle, among them the original Egyptian, along with the Admiral, Granada, Neptune and, in later years, the Lewis & Clark south of town. Much of the Arabian's ornate entryway, including the cynosural pinwheel stained-glass window, was preserved when the edifice was reincarnated as today's "I Am" Temple. (R. Miller photo)

The names mounted on those dazzling marquees as often as not betrayed the theatre's décor. Or shtick. The Colonial, on Fourth Avenue in the heart of downtown, sported a Tara-like façade but very little inside to promote Phil Harris's glorification of "that's what I like about the South."

Long before it was reborn as a triplet, West Seattle's Admiral displayed seafaring adornments well suited to a city consumed by the annual rite of summer called Seafair. Accoutrements included a roof-top mast complete with crow's nest.

The Varsity was ideally christened, given its enduring location in the University District. The name, however, exerted little influence on the theatre's nondescript motif, but perhaps inspired the excellence of its bookings from the late Fifties on.

On the other hand, the interior of the Arabian, north of Green Lake, aspired to conjure up images of the life and times of Scheherazade. Its heyday partially overlapped the era of theme-driven businesses along the Aurora Speedway like the Igloo Diner and a treasure-chest-configured filling station (which ultimately deep-sixed off the east apron of Queen Anne Hill in a slow-moving landslide). In spite of cookware giveaways prompted by the killing competition of the television juggernaut, the Arabian's faux-Persian sconces and dusty tapestries failed to outlive Walter Clark's neighboring Twin T-Ps.

(The Northgate Theatre, in any other location, might well have succeeded as the Tomahawk or the Little Bighorn given its kitschy buckskin-covered furnishings and Braves-Squaws restroom designations.)

Oddly, the 5th Avenue Theatre forsook extolling period art deco and uptown panache to offer architect R.C. Reamer's vision of the Imperial Palace's throne room in Peking's Forbidden City. Whether promoters intended it or not, the big vaudeville house beat the opening of Sid Grauman's celebrated Chinese Theatre in Hollywood by nearly a year (in 1927). But much of the exacting design work and painstaking labor was lost on a new generation of moviegoers by the time programmers like *Young Jesse James* began wasting space on the 5th Avenue's grand marquee.

The original Egyptian—the one in the U-District—probably did the greatest justice to its given name. Posher than the neighboring Neptune, this jewel among all venues north of the Canal boasted imposing urns, Anubises, along with knockoffs of the artifacts hauled out of Lower Nubia before it was flooded by the waters of Aswan High Dam. (Like Lower Nubia, the theatre was also to be swallowed up—not by a river, but by virtue of being located on the same evolving city block that included a Pay'n Save drugstore moved and expanded to better showcase Carter's Little Liver Pills, Burma-Shave and vitamins on the cheap.) Roger's mother had mixed feelings about the Egyptian's demise in the aftermath of a ferocious Jujube fight that broke out during a Saturday matinee showing of *The Long, Long Trailer* in the mid-Fifties. Scissors were required to unsnarl her ten-year-old's hair. His locks grew back, but the Ave's distinguished cinema succumbed to commercial pressures in 1959.

Other houses, however, shunned any connection between appellation and trappings. The Embassy, for example, offered the public two separate entrances on two different streets. Perhaps this was a reflection of some forgotten administration's diplomatic policy. Whatever the reason, Roger's mother for a time made liberal use of both box offices when parking her anti-consumerism son during her weekly downtown shopping expeditions. The Union Street ticket window served if she was heading for Rhodes or MacDougall's department stores; the box office on Third Avenue if she intended checking out sales at Leed's or in the Bon's bargain basement (after window-shopping at Grayson). No matter her mission, nor the entrance of choice, the Embassy offered uncounted hours with stalwart babysitters like Randolph Scott, Stewart Granger and Cornel Wilde.

So far as is known, the Blue Mouse had no connection with Seattle's rodent population. But the smallish house on Fifth was truly the mouse that roared among local cinemas in the Fifties on into the Sixties, offering exclusive engagements of such blockbusters of the era as *Around the World in 80 Days, Ben-Hur* and *Mary Poppins.*

Most of the city's prestige venues could trace their origins to vaudeville and even legitimate theatre. John Hamrick's ornate Music Hall hosted the likes of Paul Whiteman's acclaimed ensemble, along with many other big-band acts complemented by a monster pipe organ that rose to stage level from a Grand Canyon-sized orchestra pit. Rechristened the Seattle Seventh Avenue decades later, it ultimately failed to succeed as a first-run movie house, some say owing to its location on the remote eastern fringe of the city's consolidated retail hub. With the Tower Building looking on across the street, the Spanish baroque structure was battered to bits by the wrecking ball (after a good fight) in 1992. A new name, the Emerald Palace, had been ticky-tacked on the storied hall in its last years. But it wasn't enough to appeal to fickle techie tastes.

The Pantages Theatre was a prominent dot on a national circuit created by Seattle impresario Alexander Pantages. It was the last live vaudeville house in town; some claim in the entire country.* After the John Danz chain acquired it in the Thirties, its name was changed to the Palomar. It had converted to an on-and-off second-run features format by the time a *King Kong/Leopard Man* revival robbed young Mike of a week's sleep in 1953. Situated on an increasingly dowdier stretch of Third Avenue, nothing seemed to attract much of the still-flourishing uptown movie-going trade. The Palomar creaked toward oblivion hosting Junior Programs productions and an encyclopedic travelogue series emceed by Earl Prebezac. But there was little else offered to keep company with the ghosts of long-ago chorines, second bananas and forgotten sidemen.

In an age when Seattle didn't have to walk far to find all of itself, locating in the downtown retail core was vital to business success. By the end of World War I, the city's mainstream commerce had spread north to Pine and east to Sixth Avenue. And stopped. Nearly everything lying outside the golden square mile (including the much ballyhooed but, in truth, sprawling vacant lot known as the Denny Regrade) was strictly low rent.

Showman John Considine was convinced he could buck the trend. After all, his own national entertainment empire rivaled the prosperity enjoyed by Pantages. Considine opened the elegant Orpheum Theatre "way out" on Olive in 1927 as arguably the city's finest vaudeville venue. While its owner had delivered an impressive monument to the Roaring Twenties, Seattle failed to instantly grow right up to its doorstep as Considine had predicted. Not right away, at least. Its best years came with maturity after establishing itself as the region's premier switch-hitting entertainment mecca. Throughout the Fifties, and a few years beyond, Orpheum management juggled Seattle Symphony concerts with such first-rate road-show productions as *The Caine Mutiny Court Martial*, along with popular Hollywood

---

* Sammy Davis, Jr. brought down the final curtain.

fodder like *Creature from the Black Lagoon*. It wasn't unusual to find a highbrow audience applauding Milton Katims less than twenty-four hours before an army of crazed, subteen boys descended to ogle Julie Adams in a pointy one-piece through 3-D glasses. (Lord, did they ever!)

The clock was ticking for the Orpheum when the first-run showing of *Big Hand for a Little Lady* was screened in 1966. A year later, the grande dame of Seattle theatres was being reduced to rubble. The Sixties—the Fair—triggered a decades-long frenzy of architectural icon cleansing that cleared the way for creation of an urban heart mirroring the warmth of Fritz Lang's vision of *Metropolis*. (Werner Lenggenhager photos courtesy of the Seattle Public Library)

The well-mixed formula catered to a wide spectrum of the city's population. Roger and two of his cousins became aware of this when a trio of young ladies, claiming to be on an unapproved sabbatical from the Good Shepherd Home in Wallingford, pulled knives on the drop-jawed lads while they watched Alan Ladd outgun Lloyd Nolan in *Santiago* in 1956. If nothing else, the incident served as graphic proof that the shiv was the weapon *du jour* of the Rock Age.

Mike never came close to being filleted at the Orpheum. But his ears, he claimed long afterward, sustained permanent damage when Kathryn Grayson executed a remarkable clinker during her interpretation of the song "I Loved You Once in Silence" near the end of *Camelot*'s second act. Mike never returned to the venerable theatre after this August 1963 performance.

The Orpheum's fortunes waned as Northwest Releasing began rerouting more and more concerts and road shows to the Arena, the Moore Theatre and the Opera House during the World's Fair and the years immediately following the Big Carnival. At the age of forty—all too often a fatal milestone marked by vanished Seattle landmarks—the grand showplace was torn down to facilitate construction of what the underbooked town cried out for then— another hotel. The Washington Plaza.

The lacerating Roger had escaped four years earlier at the Orpheum may well have been a portent of things to come during a first-run, Saturday-night screening of *Psycho* at the Paramount. While Janet Leigh was being slashed to death in a Bates Motel shower, Roger's inaugural high school date was shredding the right sleeve of the button-down Arrow shirt he had purchased for what was destined to be their last date. Still later in the Hitchcock shocker, his high-strung and long-nailed escort managed to draw blood from the same arm in time with the attack on Martin Balsam projected on the enormous screen before them. Sensing the worst was yet to come, Roger put a vacant seat between him and the young lady prior to the movie's over-the-top climax. The move very likely saved him from further, more serious blood loss.

Less than a half-mile away, at another house Alexander Pantages built, the Coliseum was all about movies after talkies arrived. As it aged, it became Seattle's stellar first-run "B" feature theatre presenting drive-in fare under an imposing roof. If the new release was a low-budgeter, filmed in black & white or TruColor, and/or promised to offend Pauline Kael, it was almost certainly destined to debut locally at the northeast corner of Fifth and Pike. While some of its downtown competition exuded stuffiness or flaunted a signature format (early on, for example, the 5th Avenue's audiences were seated by Manchu Dynasty-garbed ushers), the Coliseum defined itself by what was playing inside. Whether showcasing rock video forerunners starring Elvis or Cliff Richards or Chuck Berry, or the antics of the Rat Pack and even the Three Stooges, the place had no pretensions. The Coliseum, mid-century, was fun and cinematically fad-driven.

The Coliseum Theatre was extensively remodeled in 1951 to bring it up to snuff with neighboring first-run houses, the Blue Mouse, Music Box and the 5th Avenue. Still, its bookings trended toward lighter-weight Hollywood fare. By 1956, three years after this photo, the likes of serious Bing Crosby vehicles had been replaced by an endless parade of creature features making the Coliseum a favorite among Seattle's pre-Gillette set. (Werner Lenggenhager photo courtesy of the Seattle Public Library)

For a period of time (roughly, *Rodan* to *Reptilicus*), the Coliseum booked a slew of horror and sci-fi stinkers. And for good reason. *Rodan* lured away the Julie Adams fan club from the Orpheum and lined it up facing south along Fifth, clear down to Pine Street, and around the corner to Sixth on opening day.

Leonard—enterprising eighth-grade entrepreneur returning with a client from a cutlery-buying spree at several First Avenue pawn shops—had, like a legion of young males nationwide, been seduced by the Japanese film's groundbreaking TV trailers. Arriving at the Coliseum just before the first showing, he was dismayed to discover the mind-boggling volume of kids queued up to see *Rodan* in TohoScope. Inspired by his earlier purchases, Leonard and his companion sidled over to the vulnerable-looking sixth-grader whose 7:00 A.M. clock-in had placed him a mere ten feet from the curtained ticket kiosk. A private demonstration of the workings of an Italian switchblade made a profound impression on the younger boy. Leonard and company were immediately allowed to, well, cut in, thereby giving them a three-hour jump on the tail of the soggy line patiently waiting to see the obnoxious bird wreak fakey havoc on the land of the rising yen.

In a time when the double bill ruled, house managers and ushers ordinarily allowed audience members to sit through however many showings of a feature they cared to endure (save for Saturday matinee mites who were rounded up and swept out before the evening's adult fare was screened). Mike and Roger graduated from high school having seen many of their favorites multiple times for the price of a single ticket. This included two—count 'em—helpings of just possibly the worst movie ever to play the future Banana Republic outlet. They sat down among what turned out to be a quarter of the student body of Garfield High School. The haphazardly integrated house laughed as non-PC one at an inadvertent (it is to be hoped) racial/horror lampoon called *Hand of Death* starring John Agar at the bottom of his seemingly depthless career. When the fifty-eight-minute cheapie was released forty-five years later on DVD (*why?*), the aging friends could only conclude that this bizarre schlockest of all schlock movies would have been banned anywhere else but at the by-now-defunct Coliseum. For seven days only.

The exclusive engagement format (granting one first-run viewing for the price of one—NO second looks) was catching on by the late Fifties at such elite downtown houses as the Music Box, the Blue Mouse and, later, the Cinerama. Farther out, however, the big suburban theatres like the Lewis & Clark and the Northgate stubbornly clung to slightly lower admissions and nearly new double bills as they battled stiff competition from the area's popular drive-ins, which were finally winning film-distribution parity.

Nevertheless, all ticket prices were trending upward. At four bits for a junior, what was a too-young-to-drive, movie-loving teen to do barely scraping by on a seventy-five-cent-a-week allowance? That's where the three-for-a-quarter, no longer elegant likes of the Embassy, the Colonial and the (Winter) Garden came to the rescue. Equal parts truant hideout, flophouse-by-the-hour and filmaholic heaven, the triple-billings offered were a grab bag that might shuffle a Western in with a spook flick and top the whole mélange off with a ten-year-old Francis the Talking Mule farce. There was little attention given to thematic consistency, or quality, at such places.

Roger escaped on a downtown-bound trolley to avoid weekend homework one Saturday in the fall of 1959. At Westlake and Fourth his eye caught the Colonial's marquee. The sighting instantly decided the rest of the day's agenda. Whistling "The Ballad of Thunder Road," he plunked down two bits at the ticket window and ran inside to catch his very favorite antihero, Robert Mitchum, star in the best car-chase actioner *ever*. (With home video technology light years away, such impulsive celluloid fixes were necessary back then because there was no telling when, or if, a favorite movie might turn up again.) One helping of moonshine-hauling wasn't enough and Roger decided to sit through the rest of the bill, which included another John Agar hoot called *Invisible Invaders*, in order to commit Lucas Doolin's cheekiest lines to memory. The UA quickie not only recycled a half hour of newsreels to pad sixty-seven dreadful minutes but drew yowls from discerning winos in the sparse audience when the '57 Ford wreck scene from *Thunder Road* was pirated to explain the recruiting of another stiff headed for the zombie army Agar and Robert Hutton were out to quell. (That's right: Hollywood had discovered the lumbering living dead long before Simon Pegg and Woody Harrelson captured a much larger fan base.)

The next year, Roger and his dad couldn't wait to line up at the 5th Avenue opening night of the widely plugged *North to Alaska*. In their excitement (Roger to see Ernie Kovacs, his dad to bond with John

Wayne), neither noticed the cryptic Sneak Preview banner outside. In fact, they were seated just in time, they thought, to catch the opening of the good-natured butt-kicker. Instead, they got *Flaming Star* for an hors d'oeuvre. An Elvis Presley movie. The credits made it *look* like a Western, but what the hell was Swivel Hips doing in it? Roger's dad threatened to storm the box office and demand a refund. (Presley wasn't close to being on the over-forty, parent-friendly list then.) Roger begged for a five-minute stay of execution. An hour and a half later, father and son remembered to finish their popcorn following the elder's grudging admission that Elvis wasn't that bad—when he packed a six-gun instead of a guitar.

Not everything ordered from the town's variable film menu was escapist fare. A Friday-night screening of *On the Beach* at the Northgate, sobering as it was, led to a memorable spree involving a fruit jar of hybrid bourbon that Leonard had surreptitiously collected following a housewarming blowout his parents had thrown the previous weekend. The film's somber tag line, "There is still time … Brother," echoed over and over out the windows of Jules' parents' '56 VW bus as it slowly cruised fifty north-end streets after the curtain. A couple of years later, Elia Kazan's *Splendor in the Grass* had the opposite effect. An early evening showing at the Neptune Theatre moved the Big Four—Mike, Jules, Roger and Leonard—to abruptly abandon plans to party hearty in West Seattle later that night. The moody film squarely struck the sensibilities of the high school seniors, and they quietly headed for their respective homes to introspect, sans alcohol, for the rest of the night.

Roger's next movie date was dumbfounded by the impact a motion picture could inflict. The screening they attended of Stanley Kramer's *Judgment at Nuremberg* had to be halted after a middle-aged audience member, a woman centrally seated in the Blue Mouse, collapsed emotionally—then physically—upon viewing a documentary insert revealing the liberation of a Nazi death camp. The footage was horrific, unprecedented in a mainstream movie to that time. Roger's date, a junior girl hailing from sanguine Sand Point, had to be clued in about the Holocaust. Roger barely knew himself. It was, after all, 1961—if not quite the age of innocence, then one sometimes blindfolded by not-so-blissful ignorance. (The young lady demanded to be taken straight home after the show. No Burgermaster—no nothing.)

Neighborhood hardtops hit hard times by the late Fifties. Drive-in theatres were the rage, peaking out at nearly 5,000 across America by 1958. Inside, the wide-screen fad had seized the country, too. It provided a tremendous draw for the big downtown palaces and newer suburban venues. But many of the modest second- and third-run houses were unable to afford, or physically accommodate, conversion to CinemaScope, VistaVision and Panavision upgrades in a world that wouldn't think of watching *The Bridge on the River Kwai* in 35mm.

The CBS Network delivered another blow by scheduling television's most-watched show, *Gunsmoke*, in the same time slot that scant years before would have found Mr. and Mrs. Saturday Night lining up at thousands of box offices nationwide. The cumulative effect was like slowly advancing cancer snuffing out, one by one, the small neighborhood theatres: the Venetian, the Hollywood, the Ballard, the Roycroft. In West Seattle, Abbott and Costello matinees, along with all other screen fare, disappeared at the Granada. Ultimately it became the Organ Loft after occasionally sputtering to life hosting live productions like Michael Druxman's lamentable staging of *Death of a Salesman* in 1962. The list of closures grew and grew.

Yet special-interest films, and the theatres that catered to them, provided niches that savvy operators were eager to cultivate. Soft-core porn began playing on First Avenue at the town's wink-wink pioneer, the Green Parrot. By the early Sixties, Russ Meyer nudies were enjoying robust runs at the Gramercy and the Guild 45th in the heart of Wallingford. (Management sternly cautioned, "No One Under 21." Yeah, sure....) Seattle's tolerance for film erotica liberalized as the decade streaked by, and newcomers to the local sexploitation market like the Green Apple and Sultan's Cinema welcomed a less-reserved generation of filmgoers embracing a broader range of uncloseted proclivities. Ailing hand-me-down houses like the Garden saw the light and converted to a heavy-duty adult cuisine featuring the likes of Linda Lovelace. The Greenwood district's Grand went XXX as the North End Cinema, as did the

Columbia (reinvented as the Rainier Cinema), until home video advancements rendered them obsolete in fairly rapid order. As the Eighties dawned, affordable VHS systems made every abode an achievable debauchitorium.

Stand-alone "art houses"—foreign and independent film showcases—fashioned an enduring and expanding market in Sixties' Seattle. L.J. McGinley—"Mac"—theatre manager and host extraordinaire, probably did more to cultivate the Queen City's taste for non-mainstream pictures than anyone who ever pitched quality celluloid in the town. Rain, snow, fog, cold and dark of night didn't deter Mac from warming up the crowds lining University Way seeking tickets to the Varsity. Always glib, charming and witty, the nattily dressed patriarch of moviedom regaled foot-weary patrons every evening with ploys like giving his solemn oath that the latest *Carry On* comedy he was screening was at least twice as funny (and, by intimation, raunchier) than the last. The era's small-budget oddities like *David and Lisa* and *Lord of the Flies*—viewed as box office poison by Danz family-controlled Sterling Theatres—played for weeks to packed houses at the Ave's intimate one-screen wonder. Rather than turn away business, McGinley would even tack on an extra late-night showing if an overflow crowd promised to return at midnight (and it always did). Then he would trot inside to man the exit and spiel his next booking to an outbound audience.

McGinley actively courted younger movie fans knowing that, once hooked on English comedies, Fellini and Tati, they would become the future life's blood of the Varsity. He admitted Roger, gratis, for three viewings of Joseph Losey's murky character study *The Servant* as the UofW junior struggled to write a coherent critique for an elective film class. Naturally, the kindness was repaid dozens of times at the ticket window as the decade wore on, and out.

Mac's salesmanship helped to rein in at least some of the mobile partying marking the high school years of the Big Four. Spending money was always tight and, when admission prices topped a dollar for students, a liberal beer budget became harder to maintain. In addition, there were only so many hours to be carved out of the shank of a promising evening; with movies, less and less time to count Oly label dots out on Alki, or to explore the raw country beyond Eastgate with a case or two of Lucky Lager in the back seat for ballast.

Yet, certain themes in the hands of the right director provoked thought and lively discussion among the lads. Some actors were even to be secretly identified with (probably none more than the babe magnet Marcello Mastroianni). Movie previews and coming-attractions posters beckoned. It came to pass that if they weren't stifling laughter at the Revival Center during a spirited Friday-night faith-healing session, they were rolling in darkened aisles watching *I'm All Right, Jack, Mr. Hulot's Holiday* or *School for Scoundrels*; or being puzzled, but captivated, by *La Dolce Vita* and *8□* ; or just plain blown away by other than beer after taking in *Breathless* from France or *The Bridge* from Germany.

They weren't alone in line. Growing numbers got hooked on the kind of quality film largely denied Seattleites for decades by Hollywood-influenced chains. The so-called art houses began, it seemed at times, showing up around town like the pods in *Invasion of the Body Snatchers*. Jim Selvidge guided the outstanding Ridgemont on Greenwood North where Seattle's hunger for foreign pictures demonstrated itself with the amazing sixty-one-week run of *A Man and a Woman*. The Edgemont in Edmonds, eventually touting a 16,000-patron mailing list, became the preeminent rapid-turnover showcase that brought the very best of international cinema to the area in head-spinning succession. Bernstein and O'Steen bought the Women's Century Club on Capitol Hill in 1968 and somehow fit the Harvard Exit Theatre inside during a loving remodel of the premises built in 1925. And in 1970, Randy Finley introduced the Ave to another indie venue, the ninety-three-seat Movie House—the modest seedling that would eventually sprout into the enormously successful Seven Gables chain.

Augmented by wide-ranging, quarterly film series sponsored by the University of Washington, it wasn't unusual to find a single week stuffed with not only stellar new releases from here and abroad, but with Marx Brothers' retrospectives and German silent-film festivals; exhibitions of Italian Neorealism; even programs featuring nothing but samurai sagas woven together with the great American Western. It was a damn fine time in Seattle to catch just about any kind of picture a true, hard-boiled movie buff could ever want to see.

But a golden age for moviegoers may well have added to the flux and ebbing of the local theatre scene. Even the mainstream venues were being radically altered or, more likely, consigned to oblivion as marquee after marquee was turned off for the last time. These closures permanently modified the nighttime face of the town; redirected the pace of leisure activities and the flow of entertainment patterns; signaled those who were conscious of such things that they no longer worked and played in a place called the Queen City. After the World's Fair—after I-5 opened all the way to the Canadian border—the winds of radical change indiscriminately blew through Seattle from every direction. And even before the scarlet MINOR stamps disappeared from their photoless driver's licenses, the Big Four began drifting—sometimes running—away from the area. Roger turned out the lights when he left for Alaska in the mid-Seventies.

Leonard and Roger had regularly haunted the heart of Seattle, and its movie houses, since meeting in the seventh grade. So it seemed only natural that they take in a show in 1970 after Leonard hit town on one of his ever-rarer visits. *M*A*S*H* was playing first-run. Industry reviews made it out to be a trendy (to some, off-putting) comedy—thus, a perfect fit at the Coliseum. Roger had grown hoarse with laughter by the time he realized his old chum wasn't cracking so much as a smile at the high jinks perpetrated by Hawkeye and Trapper John … or at Robert Altman's damning take on war. Then, a painfully slow-dawning boyhood memory jumped up and kicked Roger in the gut. He sagged back in his seat recalling that Leonard's first lieutenant dad hadn't returned from the battlefields of Korea; that the father would never see his son turn seven after shipping out in 1950.

It was the last picture they saw together for thirty-nine years. Until *Frost/Nixon*. At a multiplex in Vancouver, Canada.

# SCARING THE CRAP OUT
# OF ROBERT A. HEINLEIN

The caper grew out of an insatiable appetite for pranks and publicity, and was launched with a kitschy, Hollywood-style press release planted in Emmett Watson's *This Our City* column dated September 1, 1961.

"Not since the arch fiend Dracula walked the wind, or Frankenstein's Monster clawed his way through the bleak hills of Transylvania"—I'm scared just reading this, man—"has anything as horrifying, as spine-tingling, as nauseating confronted the likes of man." All right, crawl out from under those beds—all's clear. It's just a press agent's announcement that the World Science Fiction Writers Convention is having its grand costume bash Saturday night at the Hyatt House. Held, appropriately enough, in the Satellite Room.

Little did Emmett know about the anonymous "press agent"....

Roger's brother Gary craved the kind of ink that would earn a plug for the public relations business he hoped to get off the ground before playing out his luck as sales manager at the Swingin' 60 radio station in Everett. At about that time, while scouting a Lake City newsstand for the latest *Playboy* (interview), he discovered a copy of Forrest J. Ackerman's *Famous Monsters of Filmland*. What developed from the chance encounter was an unorthodox case of love at first sight—and a serious pledge to crash the pages of *FMF*.

During the months of woolgathering that followed, he learned of an upcoming international event scheduled over Labor Day weekend in Seattle. A plan began to jell. Past and present master of prestidigitatorial pitches, Gary convinced himself he could concoct and pull off a stunt as towering as the Second Coming of Christ would be, thereby—*somehow*—bagging two birds of paradise with a single Hail Mary.

Gary read the pulse of the seaport as well as any habitué of its ample underbelly. The Sea Hag, Pete's Poopdeck and Smokey Joe's were among the seedy haunts he frequented after the sun set. Naturally, promoters of the forthcoming World's Fair of Science (aka the Century 21 Exposition) did their level best to divert public attention from such acclaimed dens of iniquity. Day and night they overloaded the city's Linotypes selling Seattleites on the notion that humdingers like the Bubbleator would instantly transform their beloved Dogpatch on the Sound into an internationally hailed Cosmopolis (eventually, yes, sporting all the bleak charm of Gotham City). But in the very early Sixties, the town still clung to the vestiges of the century-old, yahoo-charged zeitgeist that pitted the forces of cultured piety against those of pie-eyed emancipation.

Contradictions abounded in the Queen City. For every sobering sermon on the hill at St. Mark's, there was an equally fervent search for soul after hours at the likes of Birdland. In the latter regard, no seasoned citizen could deny the existence of a salty streak, deep and often irrepressible, running from the Highlands to Holly Park and back again via White Center and Wallingford. Signs of it were everywhere. Cartooning weatherman Bob ("I'm a Milkaholic") Hale and fellow KING-TV celeb Sheriff Tex ("Snick-snick, *safety!*") Lewis enjoyed enormous popularity even as they frequently challenged sobriety on the air. None other than Bob Hope felt free to regale audiences with Bremerton ferry/fairy gags—to booming laughter—at the Aqua Theatre. Night and day, twitchy men scuttled in and out of Russ Meyer nudies screened at the Green Parrot, overcoats donned and drawn no matter the weather. In Roger's bailiwick, a thriving den of ill repute was, reportedly, still operating in the catacombs beneath an old roadhouse bearing his name out on Lake City Way. Col. Russ Schleeh had tooled around the Lake Washington hydro course at 150 mph with a silly grin on his face and a plumber's friend suctioned onto the shovel-nosed snout of the Allison-powered *Shanty I*. And the self-proclaimed Midnight Skulker was just beginning to draft plans that would soon cop *UofW Daily* headlines.... Clearly, Seattle was the kind of town that could take a joke. *Couldn't it?*

Inspiration replaced pipe-dreaming when Gary received the latest copy of *The Magazine of Fantasy and Science Fiction*. His favorite sci-fi 'zine brought astounding news that completely overhauled his original ambition to merely seek a gag write-up in *Famous Monsters of Filmland*, a publication that virtually no one older than thirteen would even see. Suddenly, there were bigger fish to fry. Seattle, he learned, had been selected as the site of the 1961 World's Science Fiction Convention (the nineteenth "Worldcon"), a time machine's tick ahead of the coming World's Fair. Not only had Robert A. Heinlein HIMSELF committed to being guest honoree[*], but none other than Forrest Ackerman, *FMF*'s creator, would be in attendance to act as unofficial greeter-cum-monster of ceremonies. The uninformed were about to learn that nothing was closer to Gary's heart than a good monster.

A once-in-a-lifetime opportunity leapt out at Gary like an unforeseen shock in a 3-D movie. In the days following, he placed fake press calls to The Nameless Ones, the local science-fiction fan club that had lobbied hard to land what was dubbed Seacon in off-the-beaten-track Seattle. He was assured that the Airport Hyatt House was, indeed, to be the site, and additionally was given a complete lowdown on the chosen weekend's schedule of events and where they were to be held in the hotel.... Lights! Camera! *Action!*

The Stuntmeister's vision quickly became clear as a Northwest morning in July. But he was still left with the nagging problem of lining up the manpower needed to assist him—stalwart lackeys who boasted a greater affinity for beer than brainwork. Most of the college set Gary had chased during a brief turn at the "U" had changed telephone numbers soon after he dropped out. The low-end media types he associated with now were either too effete, or too mercurial—or both—to want to rub shoulders with the weirdos likely to fill his monkeyshine to the brim. Gary looked closer to home. And thought younger.

---

[*] Heinlein's latest work, *Stranger in a Strange Land*, was actually elbowing its way onto some mainstream bestseller lists—quite a feat for a science-fiction novel at that time.

Send in the clowns.

To Gary's way of thinking, Roger and his merry band appeared to be diddling away the sunny season sweating and fretting. To be sure, sum-sum-summertime 1961, even for its occasional shining moment, had never blossomed into the endless bacchanal the lads had so looked forward to back in June. *Work*—and too infernally much of it—had hampered the pursuit of pleasure Mike and Roger eagerly anticipated, while the out-of-town dalliances that had distracted Jules and Leonard for a month seemed to have dulled normally ravenous appetites for beer-fueled soirees. Roger had greeted them back with open arms, along with paint brushes and the promise of a buck and a half an hour—fifty cents more than he paid himself—in hopes it would persuade the laid-back duo to help him slapdash his way through the last of his unprofitable painting commitments.

Labor Day approached and, with it, the sad inevitability of a *long* final year at the rigidly stratified country club up on East Sixty-sixth. Leonard and Jules, paint-spattered and grumbling, faced the prospect with the kind of enthusiasm reserved for a polio shot. Mike spent every waking moment squeezed between double shifts at Dick's trying his best to piece together a marketable rock 'n' roll combo. Roger was a seldom-bedded seventeen-year-old who was keenly aware that he had less than a one-in-ten chance of hooking a date for the senior prom. The realization made him edgy and drove him to bitch constantly.

The Eddie Cochran blues made them easy marks. Gary was well-versed in adolescent kvetching and was quick to recognize the prickly-heat energy bubbling just beneath the hair tonic and peach fuzz. The pack urgently needed direction, a mission supplying a vent for all that youthful magma. Gary viewed himself as the actuator who could incite a group of giddy teens to riot. With one exception.

August was racing to a close and the operation had to get under way at once. Roger was put in charge of rounding up the usual suspects for what his brother described as a few laughs at his pad—an informal assembly anointed with free beer broadly hinted to be Rocky Mountain holy water*. Only Leonard opted out, having made

---

* At the time, Coors beer was legend on the Coast, as tantalizing as casino jackpots in faraway Nevada. But Tumwater was the capital of Oly Country, and the only Coors that found its way to Puget Sound was in westbound car trunks following fun runs to, say, Wallace, Idaho.

it very clear in the past that he would never set foot in Gary's rental again. Drunken horseplay during a May Day get-together there had climaxed with the six-foot-four, two-hundred-pound host stuffing Leonard up the family-room fireplace to demonstrate a scene from the latest *Rue Morgue* horror. Leonard had dug cinders and creosote out of his scalp and ears for days, and the simmering resentment over the manhandling would never go away. Roger told his brother that Leonard had too much homework to be able to attend.

The rest showed up with bells on and whistles that craved wetting. Even when the brew *du jour* "from east of the mountains" turned out to be a case of Spokane's Bohemian Club (closeted and nearly forgotten for a year), there was no complaining because the price was right and Gary's long-suffering wife, Dixie, made outstanding deep-dish pizza. Laughs abounded, good sense languished and gradually, somehow, the freewheeling conversation came to center on the movies. Then science fiction. Sure, everybody in the room had seen *The Day the Earth Stood Still. Forbidden Planet*, too. Of course. And did anybody know, Gary asked, that *Destination Moon* had been scripted by Robert A. Heinlein? *The* Robert A. Heinlein. Jules certainly did. Indeed, one of Heinlein's early novels, *The Puppet Masters*, was a favorite read of his. Jules was rewarded with another icy-cold Bohemian—his seventh.

"You know, guys, it's a funny coincidence about Heinlein." Gary began spinning a spiel about the upcoming convention that concluded with: "And, *God*, what a gas it would be to pull off something crazy at that science-fiction powwow next weekend."

After the lads had slurred lusty approval, Gary cut to the chase and presented them with carefully drafted assignments that relied on a serious degree of commitment to the scheme. There was more noisy acclamation. Jules was up for anything. Roger was tanked— but also up for anything. Mike wasn't sure he could get out of work that night—but, oh heck, yes, he wanted in, too. Why not? By this time, neither leader nor the led knew what he was bargaining for.

The imported beer and Gary's homemade sangria ran out at the same time. Still, he wasn't able to get the party animals out of his house until after midnight. On the way to Roger's car, the teens alarmed the neighborhood with a rousing version of "The Lion

Sleeps Tonight."

*Wimoweh, wimoweh....*

Roger and Jules headed for town on a long lunch the next day, leaving an unusually bright-eyed Leonard to finish the trim on a neo-Tudor toolshed out in Blue Ridge. Jules was dropped at the Trick and Puzzle Store just up from Warshal's, while Roger headed for Olive Way and the Brocklind Costume Company with his shopping list. An hour later—tube of clown-white makeup, a cheap paste medallion and assorted odds and ends in hand—he pulled to a stop in front of Shorey's Bookstore on Third. Jules piled in holding a stack of Ace Doubles sci-fi novels and a thin paper bag clamped under his right arm.

"I got ten sheets of your flashpaper," he told Roger, "because it's pretty gimpy. The guy at the store tore off a piece of one and lit it with his cig. *Poof*—more smoke than flare. About like an old stove match."

Roger thought that over as he got on the gas to blend in with traffic. "You know, I kept the old maids out of that shipment of cherry bombs from Oregon—the ones that didn't go off at Tono." He followed the big, winking slant-eye of a '59 Chev turning right ahead of them. "There's a lot of powder in one of those things."

The demolition expert in Jules nodded sagaciously. "And you still have some of that waterproof fuse they threw in with the order?"

"Oh, yeah."

"Rog, I see great possibilities." Grinning, Jules pulled out his trademark pack of Luckies.

"I hope you feel the same about this." Roger handed his friend a scrap of notepaper covered with several lines of writing penned by a woman's hand. "That's the list of stuff Dixie wants me to buy at Saint Vincent's. Read it and weep 'cause she needs it all by tonight so she can get started."

Jules forgot his cigarette and blew out the match. "'Tux pants in Roger's size ... a woman's stiff black-velvet hat ... one black choir robe ... a woman's full coat with shiny red (satin or rayon) lining.'" Jules paused to look over at the driver. "Jesus Christ, Rog. What am I supposed to be getting?"

"Flip that over and keep reading."

After the signal turned green, the snappy little Lark convertible ate up a block of southbound Highway 99 before the two-ton Roadmaster behind it could crawl across the intersection. Inside the poky Buick, a pimply Dracula, diminutive Igor and bespectacled Dr. Death exchanged eye-rolls front and back.

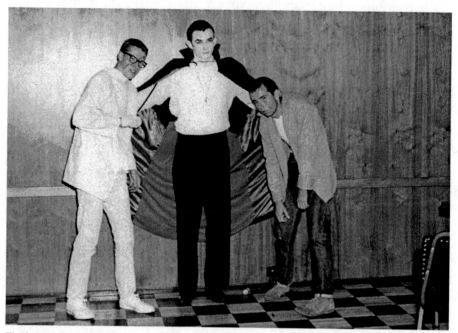

The lads — Dr. Death, the Count and Igor — reconnoiter at the 1961 World Science Fiction Convention (Seacon) held at the Sea-Tac Hyatt House. Moments later, they would unwittingly clear out the international event's masquerade ball with the help of a canned smoke bomb and an unsecured circuit panel. (JDM photo/M. Barrett Collection)

"I'll catch that barfbag in the straightaway," Gary grimly assured his sniggering passengers as the Dynaflow torque-converter whined like something straining to escape a tub of petrifying Jell-o.

"No need—this is it!" Roger continued to point at the Hyatt House sign as the black sedan wallowed right, giving its occupants a sensation akin to being astride a blue whale.

Roger requested that he and his fellow gate-crashers be dropped off at the swank airtel's front door in order to avoid incredulous looks from curious rubberneckers during the long walk in from the crowded parking lot. The vampire makeup lavishly applied by Dixie had already earned him a limp-wristed wave from a drag-racing drunk north of the Lewis & Clark Theatre. The totally unanticipated feedback had brought the sudden realization that, for once, the Weird Bunch would be indulging in bizarre public behavior without first self-medicating with buckets of beer.

Nerves and inhibitions dogged the heels of the bad doctor, Igor and the formally attired Count—but only until they stepped inside the Hyatt's lobby. They found Seacon seething with a milling throng straight off the most garish covers of *Fantastic Adventures, Astounding Science Fiction, Other Worlds* and *Planet Stories*. BEM* and their fearless foe were everywhere, their painstakingly contrived costumes doubtless appealing to the dubious taste of schlock-movie kingpin Ed Wood, who was in attendance. The otherworldly creations—along with the chutzpah required to be seen in public like that—wouldn't be matched in Seattle until the advent of Gay Pride street parades.

Gary burst through the front door looking like a traveling salesman fresh off a Pan Am flight; that is, until a closer inspection revealed his recently purchased foot apparel from Chubby & Tubby. (The press camera in his sweaty right hand further dispelled any misperception.)

"Where's Chuck Herring?" he puffed as he nervously shuffled toward his brother in the big, clunky boots entombing his feet.

"I haven't seen him," Roger promised.

"Ted Bryant?" Gary quickly scanned the entire lobby. "Isn't Ted here yet?"

"Anybody see Ted Bryant?" young Bela craned around his cape's high velvet collar to ask.

Mike and Jules shook their heads in unison and returned to gaping disbelief at a group of hobnobbing extraterrestrials.

"Isn't *any*body here from KING?" A note of indignation tinged Gary's voice.

"They'd stick out like sore thumbs if they were here," Mike piped up after adjusting his black-frame glasses. "Why, Wunda Wunda wouldn't stand out in this crowd."

Gary sighed audibly. "No Emmett Watson?"

"No Royal Brougham, either," Roger told him.

---

* *Bug-Eyed Monsters*, to committed sci-fi fiends.

"Tell Rog's brother you just saw Edward R. Murrow in a Robby the Robot getup," Jules dared Mike *sotto voce.*

Dr. Death ignored the challenge and straightened the front of his borrowed lab coat before turning all the way around to gawk at the restless, but still orderly, mob. It was clear now that the goggle-eyed, antennae-bobbing masqueraders had begun migrating, as a body, to another part of the building. When uncomfortably close-by Slan the Man ground out his Phillip Morris and joined the current, he exposed the face of a chest-high sign Mike's gaze immediately fixed on. SATELLITE ROOM, it announced. The placard provided a red directional arrow below the words for those unable to read Earthling. "Hey, look," he said, nudging Jules. "These cats are on the move. Must be the bash is starting."

The friends began to drift with the flow, unaware that the brothers were involved in a lively conversation behind them. Gary had fessed up to salting Watson's column with his colorful prose, then admitted to mailing unauthorized convention press kits to local television and radio stations. Ever a glutton for publicity—good or bad, it seemed—Gary, in his zeal, had not reckoned with the event being held on a weekend—a long holiday weekend, at that. In those days, most of the area's news outlets were locally owned, excepting, of course, the Hearst-skippered *Post-Intelligencer.* Perhaps as an outgrowth of a less gun- and bomb-obsessed Seattle, or just because holidays meant more then, news staffs were generally cut to the bone on Saturdays and Sundays, or during major stay-at-home rites like Thanksgiving. Maybe radically different tastes explained the era's narrower nose for the gory and sensational on days off. At any rate, a clamoring press corps wouldn't be storming the Hyatt House that evening, and Roger was doing his level best to deliver that news to his disappointed, but ever-calculating, brother.

"Say, how about we kidnap Heinlein ... maybe leave him blindfolded under that Space Needle thing they're building? At least the cops would find out about it."

Roger had to stand on tiptoes to try and neutralize the four-inch height advantage Gary's thick-soled gunboats gave him. "And you can be sure the police would find out who was behind it. You really don't need that to happen, Gary. Not again."

"Well then, what about Forry Ackerman? We could snatch him—put him aboard the *Kalakala*, or something. He's a funny guy."

"Nobody's funny enough to go along with that." Roger brushed at sweat forming on his brow and, so doing, smeared his painted-on widow's peak into something that looked like Bill Haley's spit curl. "No, Gare, we're here to snap some pictures, maybe grab this Ackerman guy's autograph—*if* we can find him—and then get the h-e-double-toothpicks outta here before we have to pay admission."

"But, Rog, who's going to remember that?" Gary was close to pleading now.

"*We* will. The four of us. Till we're old and gray—with no prison time on our records." It wasn't a persuasive argument until Roger remembered the parcel pressed tight against the folds of his restitched choir-robe cape. He lifted the brown paper sack high enough for Gary to see. "There might be plenty of memories inside this."

"What's—?"

"—I think it's the attention-getter you wanted. Jules calls it the Hills Brothers' stink bomb: a wad of flashpaper sprinkled with the loose powder out of a dozen two-inchers." Roger unfurled the patchwork cape for effect. "We enter *from* a cloud, we exit *in* a cloud. Mainly, we exit."

Gary gave the bag a dubious once-over. "Does that thing have much pizazz?"

"It *might* blow out the back wall." Roger concealed the parcel behind his back as a cross between the Gray Mouser and Peter Pan hurried by. "I don't really know because it's the kind of thing you can't rehearse in advance."

"You know, we could always turn out the lights after your bomb goes off," Gary scripted in an inwardly directed voice.

"Look, you find the switch and we'll—"

"—You guys *gotta* see this!" From out of nowhere, Mike was suddenly panting at their side. Beckoning wildly, he dashed off in the direction he had come.

One peek inside the open double doors answered a seldom-broached question asking how well science-fiction conventioneers could dance, given the opportunity. Owing to the five-to-one male-female attendance ratio, it was evident that not many had ever had the opportunity. In this case, however, mere demographics certainly didn't dampen high spirits. The twenty or so couples who had taken to the dance floor had immediately formed an uninhibited conga line. The astute soul acting as disc jockey responded by replacing a seven-inch reel of Theramin favorites with a taped collection of Carmen Miranda's greatest hits. As Gary and the others trespassed, members of the serpentine were yielding to cosmic rhythms as the portable Webcor's speakers belted out "The Wedding Samba".

"I bet they'd get busted in Windermere for doing that," Jules cracked before gushing laughter wouldn't let him talk anymore.

Gary grew impatient as the shock value of the sight began wearing itself out and motioned the lads against the nearest wall to film them à la Jimmy Olsen. Then he donned his sport coat backwards and unpocketed the Glenn Strange monster face he had owned since his own high school epoch. Mike got a quick lesson in how to operate the Graflex and popped three flashbulbs capturing the brothers menacing one another in sappy grandstanding poses. For all their mugging, a phony Transylvanian count and a big guy lummoxing around in a fakey Frankenstein mask were a waste of film compared to the essay possibilities tripping all over the Hyatt's dance floor. The novice photog inserted another bulb and summoned the nerve to ask Gary if he could take a few shots of the fruitcakes who had escaped from a Rod Serling hallucination.

"It's gonna need more film," Gary determined following a quick inspection. "I'll find a dark corner and put in a new roll." He pulled off the mask and ordered his troupe to stay put.

They stepped well back from the sidelines and resumed ogling the bow-tied, slide-ruled day crowd that had gone galactic for the affair. Still believing he could isolate Robert Heinlein's face from the mother lode of geekdom, Jules stood on a folding chair scanning each alien until, a moment later, he did recognize someone. He hopped down fingering a deserted recess across the way for Roger to see. "Your brother wants something. Over there."

They focused on Gary's flapping arm but were unable to decipher the meaning of his wild gesturing until the friends began pointing at one another. "I'm guessing he wants you to go see what's up," Roger deduced for the posture-challenged one.

"Why me?" Jules asked with unconcealed suspicion.

"I have no idea," Roger sighed.

"He's only forty feet away. Couldn't he come tell us?"

Roger stroked his lacquered locks. "That's not his style."

Mike repositioned the little pillow under Jules' surplused Army shirt in order to lend a touch of Quasimodo to the proceedings. "Stick out your tongue and tell him to find you some bells to ring."

Jules mumbled a Latvian obscenity. "Tico Tico" was blaring out across the Satellite Room as he hobbled away, in character, rubbing his collodion scar and drooling for effect.

Frankenstein's creation swept the oncoming Igor into the dark corner with him, and instantly they vanished into the Hyatt's own time warp behind a folding, ceiling-high partition. Mike and Roger had only just begun to fret when Gary reappeared, alone now, and covered the intervening distance in ten monstrous steps.

"Where's Jules?" Roger wanted to know.

"Inside a service pantry I found," his brother huffed. "The fuse box for the ballroom just happens to be in there. As soon as your buddy finishes his cigarette, he's going to douse the lights."

"All of them?" Mike asked.

"Hell, I don't know," Gary admitted with a shrug. "We figured the biggest switch ought to do it. Nothing was labeled."

"So what's our timing look like?" Roger pressed.

Gary put down the camera to consult a dead uncle's Gruen Curvex now wrapped around his wrist. "In just about two and a half minutes Jules will kill the lights for fifteen seconds. You'll set off your fog bomb during the blackout, giving us a wall of smoke to burst through when the lights come back on. *That*, my friends, oughta tan some Martian skivvies." Something in Gary's bright eyes made the lads feel clammy. Theirs was not a novel reaction to that look. "*Cool*, huh?"

"S-o-o-o," Mike stalled to steel himself, "what do I do?"

The Graflex was up off the floor and in Dr. Death's hands in a heartbeat. "*You* are in charge of getting it on film. Take as many of Frankie and Drac as you can—different angles, action shots, *every*thing. Use the viewfinder like I showed you." Mike stood rigid while Gary transferred the last of the flashbulbs from his coat pockets to the smock's. Then it was back to the Gruen watch for another time check. "Okay, men, we've got … oh, about ninety seconds. Rog, set that thing off *behind* everybody so we grab the whole audience when they turn around to see what's going on."

Without pausing, Gary refitted the rubber mask and drifted away to size up possible approaches for his sneak attack on the unsuspecting crowd. Mike took to a chair and plopped the press camera in his lap for a final inspection. Roger subconsciously, if inaptly (it would soon develop), hummed the theme from television's *Mr. Lucky* as he fumbled for the Jade Pagoda matchbook in his vest. He was unaware that rivulets of sweat pouring off his scalp were streaking the clown-white makeup covering his forehead, giving his pallid face an aspect more in keeping with Batman's nemesis, The Joker. Gradually, he reined in frazzled nerves. After all, there was ample time, still, to activate the coffee-can smudge pot—about thirty seconds, he guessed, from the instant he lit the fuse on the device he had carefully lifted out of the sack.

After counting to fifty, Roger struck a match. The fuse instantly sizzled to life and the pyromaniac vampire crept forward concealing the container as best he could in the folds of the cape. Per instructions, he placed it in back of the cheap seats; as it turned out, dead center in a makeshift aisleway allowing the revelers to slip through the forest of folding chairs. Mike, taking the fuse-lighting to signal kickoff time, hoisted the camera and moved toward the crowd shouting, "Make way! *University District Herald!*"

Gary was out of the blocks simultaneously, lumbering in his brother's direction like an elephantine sleepwalker. Roger found himself recovering from a violent collision with a stout, very Caucasian woman deeply immersed in the role of the Black Priestess of Varda: a lady who, upon laying Theda Bara shiners on Gary, wanted—in the worst way—to get close to Hollywood's most enduring monster. She moved briskly, for all her heft, and appeared oblivious to the fact that her outer tinfoil brassiere was working loose from the nigrosine-dyed flannel tent beneath it. "Hi-ya, Frank!" she trumpeted after she had literally hit the mark, and clung.

A muffled "hunh?" escaped from behind the green and black false face as the suddenly immobilized Gary sought to train the mask's tiny eyeholes on the obstruction. "Ar-r-r-g," he threatened the immovable mass of nylon wig pressed to his chest.

A hefty lady who dared pass for the Black Priestess of Varda likely hadn't modeled for cover artist Allen Anderson's original painting. No matter. Aspiring look-alikes for Dracula and Frankenstein's monster at the 1961 World Science Fiction Convention's grand masquerade ball weren't so hot either. (R. Miller Collection)

Undeterred, the Black Priestess looped her cat-o'-nine-tails around the Creature's neck, drawing him in closer to purr, "Big Boy, how about you and me trip the light fantastic?"

Gary knew that the burning fuse was well on its way to glory, and the next "ARRRRRG!" he snarled was fraught with heavy menace and rising anger.

The couple *had* joined in a dance of sorts, as Gary drove the woman backward toward his dumbstruck brother and The Bomb. He was unable to see anything now save the missed cue and a potential public-relations debacle to follow. "Let go of me, you bimbo!" he cried and gave the startled Vardan a rude shove toward a line of folding chairs.

The spurned woman bounded three steps in reverse, far enough for the spiked heel of her right slipper to meet the side of the coffee can with the impact of a pro football kicker's toe. Little Boy, with only millimeters of fuse left to burn, skated lickety-split down the crease between seats leading to the dance floor. The whirling container was a double-take away from mingling with the conga line when it T-boned a plastic lizard's foot its owner had carelessly thrust out into the aisle. The can, still upright, ricocheted ninety degrees into the seated mass of inhumanity. There it lodged under the chair occupied by a Flash Gordon wannabe just as the last of the hissing red fuse turned to ash.

Flash looked up from examining the Bakelite ray gun he had purchased at the downtown Kress store on Tuesday. A curious *thusp* sound, followed by what felt vaguely like a fist striking the underside of the seat beneath him, brought him to his feet. He spun about and instinctively leveled his prop weapon on the five-foot-four Klaatu directly behind him. The men had only enough time to blink at one another before the first billows of dense smoke engulfed them.

"We've been gassed!" cried the Klaatu from St. Paul. His revelation was answered by the burst of a flashbulb and a storm of shocking profanity. The conga line rear-ended itself to a stop.

*Then* the lights went out.

"Oh, dear." In the abrupt darkness, Virginia Heinlein stepped back from the Admiral hi-fi console and frowned. The power outage had interrupted radio station KXA's final selection of its broadcast day, Mahler's *Das Lied von der Erde*. "I wonder what could have happened," she mused. She felt her way to the westward-facing picture window in the economy suite at the rear of the Hyatt House. After locating the draw cord, Mrs. Heinlein parted the drapes and studied the gathering darkness outside. "Odd, but the neon sign next door is on."

Her husband rose, with Naval Academy decorum, from a paper-strewn desk and stroked his short-cropped moustache. "I expect this has something to do with the evening's festivities."

The celebrated author joined his wife at the window.

The men standing inside the front door watched the black Buick Roadmaster galumph across the parking lot, turn left and barge its way into northbound traffic.

"You think that bunch had something to do with this?" the janitor asked King County Deputy Knut as the corpulent sedan gathered speed on Highway 99.

"The big guy driving that tub has been on everybody's most-wanted list at one time or another. But, Jesus, I don't know about this." Knut turned all the way around to retest the limits of credulity by looking over the alien infestation milling aimlessly in the eerie haze seeping after them into the lobby. "It isn't like we're hurtin' for plenty'a other suspects. Besides, none of those four goofballs had been drinking. That's why I let 'em go."

The custodian kept his eye on the Saturday-night traffic navigating the concrete lifeline binding Tacoma and Seattle. "Where'd you know him from?"

"He had a little weekly newspaper in Federal Way a few years back. It's gone now—bust—but not his reputation down that way."

"Bad?"

The deputy grunted. "Gary rented a pad on the north end of Steele Lake across from a little bible camp." Knut wiped his chops to conceal an involuntary smile. "Christ, we must'a been called out there once a week by the neighbors on account'a the kick-ass parties he threw. Helluva host, though. He always had a cold beer ready for the investigating officer."

The janitor missed the part about the cold beer when he turned away from the door. "I thought Statz would be here by now," he fretted.

"He the guy you phoned about getting the juice back on?"

The other man nodded. "He was the only electrician I could raise tonight. I guess most is outta town havin' a good time. Lucky for me Statz calls the Midway Tav home."

"He have any idea what the trouble is?" Knut chomped down on a fresh stick of Juicy Fruit and eyed the pair of widely spaced, battery-operated emergency spots providing meager light to the jam-packed lobby.

"All he knows is that everything here is on the fritz—lights, TVs, ice machines, air conditioners—the whole shootin' match. I sure hope he gets here P.D.Q." He scratched at a patch of dandruff as he watched the Girl in the Golden Atom walk by, arm-in-arm with the disheveled Black Priestess of Varda.

The deputy leaned over to whisper, "Add these space cadets to your list. The whole bunchuv'ems on the fritz in my opinion."

The custodian didn't hear that, either. "You know, I can't figure it out."

"Yeah?"

"I mean, that smoke in the convention room doesn't smell like burning insulation—that scorched, rubbery kinda stink. You know. No, this here is more like a Roman candle—a real big one—went off in there. Go figure."

"I'm not even gonna try," Knut told him as he flexed broad shoulders, causing his leather accessories to creak. "Maybe your manager can get to the bottom of it. He oughta be here real soon, too. Tell him if he finds somebody he wants to press charges against, I'll come back."

"You headed for the Spanish Castle?"

"It's Saturday night, isn't it?" Knut thought better of mentioning his weekly, off-the-record habit of hassling neckers at Saltwater Park along about midnight. "That kinda action suits me better than this geek show."

"And it's on the right planet, too," the janitor quipped after an Illustrated Man had passed.

The Buick was north of the Duwamish Drive-In now. No one had spoken a word since fleeing the Hyatt House.

Robert sniffed the air in the corridor and turned to his wife when they reached the fire exit a few doors down from their room. "I'm getting a whiff of July Fourth out here." He smiled at the notion. "Bob Bloch warned me that these events occasionally become imbued with the gusto of a toga party."

"So does he. Occasionally." Mrs. Heinlein laughed and found her husband's hand. "What a fine opportunity to go exploring."

Wide-eyed, the couple strolled through the open door into a fine summer's night.

# ANOTHER DAY AT THE RACES

The slowest way to the track was almost the fastest then, driving from the Montlake district south toward Renton as far as Lake Washington Boulevard took the motorist.

At first they weren't in a hurry. The weather was clear and languid, working on being hot. Better yet, it was a Saturday, the beginning of a real weekend for a change. Mike had found a hand willing to fill his fry cook's slot at the Dick's in Wallingford. Roger was dragging his feet on a new painting project—a garage—out in the Golden Gardens area: a job already shaping up to be another dollar-an-hour grind.

Neither of them had enjoyed a proper day off since that last dismissal bell rang down the curtain on their junior year at Roosevelt High, home of the Big Stick. The unasked-for painting sideline had mushroomed into a six-, even seven-day-per-week, dawn-to-dark treadmill that, most nights, found Roger unconscious in his bed by 10:00. Mike had been stymied trying to save enough of his income to buy either a car or one of the new Wurlitzer electric pianos that had become the rockers' rage and required a set of wheels to haul anywhere. But his unlicensed and autoless parents insisted he pass expensive traffic combat lessons at Kirshner Driving School before even thinking about getting a learner's permit, allowing his buddies to broaden his street smarts. And, anyway, it seemed that Jules and Leonard had been absent most of the fleeting summer, off corrupting wholesome Lutheran girls at a retreat in the foothills up near the pass.

The preamble to a ripsnorting senior year hadn't been much to shout about. Not until today.

Roger bassed up the radio to give more twang to Duane Eddy's theme from *Ring of Fire*. The week's charts fostered more air time for some pretty good instrumentals by the Exotics, Wailers, Ventures and "Last Night's" very cool tunesmiths, The Mar-Keys. Del Shannon pulverized hi-fi speakers with "Hats Off to Larry," while the Everlys' over-the-moon harmony immediately kicked in after thirteen drummers pounded out the opening of "Temptation." Innovation was creeping into a few of the titles, too, like the flipside of the Gambler's "Moon Dawg," "LSD-25." What was that all about? No matter, for there was far too much Linda Scott, Ann-Margret, Pat Boone and Andy Williams infecting the charts with pap pop to match last summer's stellar lists of hits. Where was another "Muleskinner Blues," a "Rockin' Matilda"* or "Only the Lonely"? For Pete, even an "Alley Oop"? Ye gods, the Fab Fifty was on the skids midway through 1961.

Every radio station had jumped on the Mantle-Maris homerun bandwagon as the summer wore on. DJs were actually cutting into songs to announce each HR hammered by one of the two sluggers—as if there were a snowball's chance either of them would break the Babe's season record that had stood since the Twenties. They were killing time yakking about it now on KAYO, and that earned nearby KQDE a listen. With Seafair starting next weekend, what were the New York Yankees to a Seattle lad with roostertail froth coursing through his veins? The Lake Washington route they had chosen to take today was a tantalizing appetizer that would have to tide them over until the thunderboats arrived to stir up the placid water below them.

The southernmost third of the lake came into view after they cruised under the western end of the one-and-only floating bridge, not long ago the best place there was to view the *Slo-Mo* Flying Start. Farther ahead lay the Stan Sayres Memorial Pits, soon-to-be hostel for two dozen of the fastest boats on earth. The sighting inspired a lively debate weighing the strengths of the Muncey-driven *Miss Thriftway*, now camouflaged as the *Miss Century 21*, against those of the Musson-piloted "Green Dragon" (Roger endorsed the latter by virtue of owning one of the U-40's 1958 National Champion buttons handed out by Ole "Did It Again" Bardahl himself). The

---

* The rousing send-up of "Waltzing Matilda" was the only hit recorded by The Swags hailing from Bellingham.

anticipation was almost enough to call up mothballed bikes from storage to drag homemade wooden hydro models around the nearest playground one more time. Almost.

The next timecheck on Cutie Radio broke the spell. It was less than a half hour till the parade to the post. The expedition's leisurely pace gave way to the whirring complaint of the Ford transmission's slipping bands. Roger veered west and joined southbound Empire Way just below the Rainier Avenue divide. He took his chances on an untried course that skirted the Earlington Golf Club and was rewarded with clear sailing onto the grounds of venerable Longacres Race Track, just as his Uncle John—cab driver and pony aficionado extraordinaire—had guaranteed.

Signs led them to a sprawling parking area on the grassy acreage north of the track. The 1953 Customline four-door blended in perfectly with the clunkers belonging to the grandstand trade. Under any other circumstances, the lads likely would have lingered a few minutes to take in the unfamiliar territory surrounding them. It was a day that invited drinking in fresh country air while admiring the lushness of rich valley farmland stretching, with almost no commercial impediments, all the way to the little town of Kent neither of them had ever visited. Just then, however, a lone, mustering bugle announced a sonorous voice that distance and the track's primitive p.a. system reduced to the kind of garble that had befuddled the train travelers at the beginning of *Mr. Hulot's Holiday*. It all sounded very important.

In spite of sweating mightily after running about a block, they opted not to shed coats and knotted ties. The costume, they had calculated (rounded out by conspicuous copies of the *Daily Racing Form* Uncle John had procured from Joe Bernbaum at Green's Cigar Store on Third), was the key to being admitted. Word had it that the minimum age to get in was eighteen. Mike, seven months short of the requirement, was the senior of the pair. Their unsuccessful attempt to catch Tempest Storm at The Rivoli had been a stretch, granted. But to be turned away from a pari-mutuel window at seventeen when one's money was just as good as Methuselah's...?

Roger had broached the subject with Uncle John who, smiling, flicked the ash from his L&M and asked his nephew to consider the unlikely existence of Longacres in a state where women couldn't sit at a bar, where it was illegal to sell red meat on Sunday, and where the odd Irish Sweepstakes ticket was peddled with more stealth than dealing firearms inside the big house at Walla Walla. "Just take as much dough as you can afford to lose" had been his unsolicited advice. "Don't tell your parents where you're going and, for Chrissake, never use the word *graft* within a mile of the place." Packing copies of the daily dope sheet had been a brilliant afterthought, reasoning that busy hands might not appear to be shaky hands to a vigilant ticket seller.

The lusty ladies of the city's premier burlesque house perform a family-rated revue on wheels for the 1954 Seafair Parade. It was an era when Seattle seemed far less priggish about acknowledging the randy side of its persona. (Werner Lenggenhager photo courtesy of the Seattle Public Library)

Mike, long the acknowledged master of negotiating First Avenue beer buys for his pals, recommended his friend keep eyes glued to the racing form as they entered. "Try to look like you've been here a hundred times before," he told Roger who, at that moment, could have sworn he saw a ten-year-old girl—but *maybe* a midget with curly blonde locks—in the line ahead. It was while Mike was scanning his own copy that epiphany blindsided his friend; Roger found that he could have made better sense of the bettor's bible had it been printed in upside-down Greek. The names and records of trainers and jockeys meant little to him; the crowded numbers handicapping the horses even less. He stared at the form anyway.

They were *suctioned* into the building.

"I coulda been reading a *Little Lulu* comic book for all that guy …" Roger's words trailed off as he began to notice the sea of faces on all sides. Everywhere he looked were body and voice doubles for Leo Gorcey and Huntz Hall—in fact, every one of the Bowery Boys seemed to have a stand-in at Longacres that day. And the women? Suffice to say, the smart I. Magnin set was sequestered from the riffraff in the members-only clubhouse. The shutouts seemed committed to wearing too-small pedal pushers and chewing gum like hungry rabbits feeding on clover.

1933's House Bill 59, endorsed by State Representative Warren G. Magnuson, was signed into law by Governor Clarence Martin on March 13. Its enactment overturned part of the state's 1909 ban on gambling and legalized pari-mutuel betting on horse races. Less than six months after Olympia's approval, Longacres Racetrack opened west of Renton to kick off a flourishing 59-year run. The aerial photo featured was taken in 1955. (Ken Alhadeff Collection)

They arrived too late to bet on the first race. Relieved of the pressure to wager, the chums reacted like babes turned loose in toyland. Oh, the spectacle of it all, like 50,000-volt electricity; the roar of the crowd as forty hooves scuffed the manicured racetrack into a storm of flying dirt clods; a photo finish, to boot—why, it was the most exhilarating form of entertainment either of them had ever beheld. It left them craving—*drooling* for—a piece of the action. But using what plan of attack when their only tool read like hieroglyphics?

It was at this point that dormant memory tapped Roger on the shoulder. His dad—long ago a teenage cowboy from Eastern Washington—had several times related how he and a cagey brother-in-law from Ann Arbor had come up against a similar situation at the track in New Orleans during the Forties. Deliberately misleading consensus information (they learned later) put them deep in the hole after the first three races. Quick, they had to figure another way to bet on the local ponies, or else call it an afternoon. Both of the men claimed rural roots and had logged a lot of hours on horseback, and they wound up using their equine knowledge to visually inspect what they wagered on while the chargers were being outfitted in the paddock. By picking the most unperturbed, yet strongest-looking of the lot, they had cleaned up on the last seven races—or so countless retellings had the listener believe.

Roger couldn't recall the last time he had even been near a real-life horse. It might have been during a fourth-grade visit to the Shetland pony concession at Woodland Park, for all he knew. To their credit, both lads had grown up being keen admirers of Silver and Trigger and so, at the very least, knew what a well-behaved, housebroken steed looked like. But no matter, any system was better than no system at all. As they worked their way through the crush of milling railbirds, Mike got a severe look from a guy with William Bendix attitude when he asked the stranger for directions to the "oatburner exhibit." That was all he got from the man. Eventually, they found their way to the paddock on their own, well before the second race.

The standards governing best-bet selections may have seemed half-baked at first. But, in no time, their formula was approaching the kind of scientific methodology a person could bank on. Mike and Roger quickly determined that they didn't like—and wouldn't wager on—horses wearing blinders. Ponies decked out in them seemed edgier than the others, even unruly at times, and attracted the biggest clouds of flies, besides. Nags who relieved themselves in the paddock or worse yet during the parade to the gate were exempted from consideration because they might not be edgy enough. Calm but certainly not docile horses—and here there was admittedly a fine line—were favored over nervous numbers throwing heads and/or hissy fits. And classy color coordination of the jockey's silks and his mount's gear didn't hurt a prospect's cause, either.

From then on, through the tenth and final race, they shuttled amid the blended odors of leather, manure and liniment, and the headier aroma of cash being shoveled into the two-dollar ticket windows. In between, they critically eyed the ever-changing tote board across the track from the grandstands. Uncle John had counseled against betting on long shots, explaining, "Never buy into a high-flier unless you have the inside dope." The lads translated his advice to mean that a wager exceeding three-to-one odds was chancier than disarming one of the undetonated German bombs still being unearthed around London ... four-to-one *only* if the no-pooping-blinders-snappy-dresscode factors meshed perfectly. John had also discouraged trying to pick winners: "Don't try to be a hero—spread the risk a little. A payoff on a place bet, even a show sometimes, is a helluva lot better than going home with an empty wallet."

There was more to the crash course. Reliable jockeys were important, too, it developed. Uncle John had dropped the names of DeAlba, Frey and Simonis before being called away to pick up a fare at the main gate of Fort Lawton. That and everything else he had imparted to them was systematically fed to the UNIVAC-challenging database they were building for use on the Big Day.

They bet on carefully profiled mounts bearing such handles as Mr. Petition, Lunch Hour and Glitter's Ghost. And in rolled the money—nothing Midas would have wet himself over, to be sure, because sometimes the net was as little as seven dimes and never more than three dollars. But at the rate of a couple of bucks per hour, on average, it was more than both of them were earning that summer busting their humps. It was heady stuff, truly intoxicating: the kind of easy money that could turn the head of a solid, middle-class Seattle kid.

Once, Roger let barefaced greed lead him astray. Pulse pounding, eyes blinded by diamond dust, he gave into reckless hunch and put two dollars on the nose of a horse named Mad Money in the seventh. The chestnut filly was a thirty-to-one long shot who not only faded out of the money to finish tenth in a ten-horse field but, according to rumor, was still running in the direction of Factoria and the Sunset Drive-In. Shamed and sobered, Roger got back into the reliable groove and recouped his loss, and then some, by putting his deuce on Burnt Hat in the eighth (the jock's purple-and-gold togs had sealed the deal).

The pace was, at once, invigorating *and* demanding. Mike was the first to succumb to the hunger pangs gnawing at each of them, and it required less than six minutes to chow down what Roger, for the rest of his life, would remember as the best roast-beef sandwich he ever ate. They attacked the jaw-popping Dagwoods standing outside the Eddie Arcaro Room, pacing as they munched, stifling what any other day would have been a powerful temptation to try and score one of the giant, four-bit take-out beers sold at the bar. Not today, however, because today was devoted exclusively to the adrenaline-injected glory there was in outwitting The Man. No matter that Longacres was a rickety vestige of the Depression, thrown together in less than a month back when. This was as audacious as knocking over the gambling palaces of Vegas *and* Reno—a scheme carried out to perfection by two sly young dogs every bit as ballsy as Danny Ocean and all his Rat Pack cronies put together.

In the end, they had cashed winning tickets from eight of the nine races played. That cleared them just over sixteen dollars after expenses: admission, gas, food, odds and ends. Mike netted eighty cents more than his partner in crime. But nobody was counting as they walked on air for the parking lot. Judging from the throwaways forming a thick, multicolored carpet in front of the two- and five-dollar windows, they must have been the only plungers to come out ahead that day. Too bad, they agreed, that winning pari-mutuel tickets couldn't be kept as souvenirs to show the folks back home (actually, to everybody *but* their folks). Hey, though, a pocketful of dough was proof enough of their skill, and the pride of beating the house felt even better than the green and all those dimes.

They hurried for town with their loot and newfound status: up 99/Marginal Way past Boeing and yet-to-be-cherished landmarks that hadn't gone missing yet, like the Circle Tavern and Hat 'n' Boots Texaco. It was the kind of summer Saturday the Greater Seattle people liked to crow about, and it was early enough in the century that the majority of a person's time wasn't preassigned and didn't have to be accounted for. They were young men of means that day in

July, winners and bon vivants in Robert Hall sports coats and inch-wide ties. The Runyonesque ambiance of the late afternoon escorted the Ford up Fourth Avenue, across Yesler, on the way to celebrate the next best thing there was to breaking the bank at Monte Carlo.

The ticket lady at the Colonial Theatre yawned out her glass speaking hole as they drove by. The abundant meter parking on the street attested to the fact that virtually the entire downtown retail core had, by 5:00 P.M., closed for the balance of the weekend. There were exceptions, of course, especially if one went west toward the tawdry edge of the city, along First. But it was far too light for the jaunty teens to even consider trolling Skid Road. Another sport of kings was foremost on their minds now that they had conquered the morning line.

A half-empty trolley whispered by the car after Roger had nosed into a parking place ten steps from the Fourth Avenue entrance to Ben Paris. They sauntered, joints loose, down the split-level staircase like extras edited from the final cut of *The Hustler*. Then it was through the heavy brass-trimmed swinging doors and down the last short flight into blue tobacco fog to the level where the action was.

Men who used only one-syllable monikers didn't bother to look up at the pair who had paused to warily eyeball the scene from the second-to-last step. Every one of the immaculate, green-felt-dressed tables—billiards, snooker and straight pool—was occupied. The ball boy, brush in hand, was poised everywhere at once to groom playing surfaces and set up the next rack. For a quarter.

The tables drawing the best-attired players and audiences appeared to be meccas for the money matches. Elsewhere, *Honeymooners* types played with house sticks, didn't call shots and mainly competed for beers shooting lowbrow games like Screw Your Buddy. But everybody and his buddy conformed to the code of deference that hung over the hall as heavily as the nicotine-laced smoke. There was no sound but the tap of cue tips, the clack of balls and the click of overhead bead counters; no feminine distractions but for what little could be heard of Miss Toni Fisher's hurt escaping the Sportsman's Cocktail Lounge.

It was Roger who tired first of being a spectator, observing in a low voice as he nodded at the nearest billiards table, "I'll never dig how you make a game outta shooting three balls at no pockets."

"Wanta challenge?" Mike had spotted a pair of young men playing Stars and Stripes at a distant table. "Over there."

Roger saw them, too, and nibbled his lower lip after noticing their forearm Navy tattoos. "Ugh, what say we hit the Ball and Rack on the way home—I mean, if you're still up for a game by then."

There was silent agreement to the plan, and the two of them stepped off the last stair. Leaving the gaming area, they skirted the coin-sprinkled trout pond and set out for the tobacco counter. In spite of the Marlboro Man's popularity, Fatima was still the best-selling cigarette at Ben Paris. Here, an amazing assortment of tobacco products, from Turkish Maltepes to English snuff, were arranged for ogling under beveled glass and inside polished teak display cases.

"How about a couple of those?" Mike asked the watery-eyed concessionaire who responded by dipping into a box of fifteen-cent coronas on the counter. "And maybe we could cash these in for folding."

Roger added his handful of dimes to Mike's and smiled hopefully.

"Been to the races?" the bow-tied vendor asked with little effort given to hiding his indifference.

"Yeah, and did *good*," Mike answered cheerfully.

Two deft fingers instantly went to work on the puddle of silver coins, adding a pair at a time to a plastic counting tube. There were enough to fill a green paper dime roll, plus a dollar more and a few odd left over.

"A fin and an ace okay?" the money-changer proposed.

Roger butted in with, "Ones would be better," after quickly reviewing his *Peter Gunn* education in currency talk. "Please."

Six singles were fanned onto the countertop before the tobacconist separated the cost of the cigars from the fifty-cent remainder. Mike took the cash, handed Roger three of the bills and one of the coronas, and started to pocket his half. When he caught the direction of the man's eyes, he paused. "Those're yours." The duo of dimes tinkled into a little china cup beside the antique NCR machine.

Then Roger summoned the courage to ask, "Can you tell us what kind of dinner we can get here?"

Moist eyes drifted toward the Westlake side of the storied establishment. "I happen to know today's special's corned beef and cabbage. Can'cha smell it?"

Roger could now and blanched at the thought of his least favorite dish on earth.

"Cod, too, I think." The counterman frowned. "Boiled, probably. Maybe mixed with macaroni." The frown grew grave. "Guy that cooks here weekends thinks he's a seafood chef ... in another life, maybe."

They both thought they noticed the man shudder. "Wouldn't want to miss a meal like that," Mike told him with such sincerity that his friend's jaw dropped. "But it looks like we'll have to on account of it's time to move 'n' groove." He winked at Roger before turning back. "Say, how 'bout some matches?"

After laughing their way back up the stairs to Fourth, they decided to treat themselves to a repast worthy of the occasion—not Canlis or Trader Vic's, certainly, but at some place not far down the hall from first cabin. Roger had been impressed with the club sandwich he and his mother had split a couple of years before at a nearby restaurant called Von's. Mike was up for anything that figured to be a square meal and, leaving the car where it was, they ambled south toward the Pay'n Save sign a block and a half away.

Following a two-minute wait, they were escorted by an aloof maître d' to the very rear of the far-from-overflowing Prohibition-era relic that had been popular with Roger's folks back in the day of the flapper. Hunger decided the friends against a risky gamble on wangling a pair of Zazaracs off the adult, before-dinner cocktail list. A starchy waiter seemed unwilling to take notice of them until they had heaped all of their cash out in the open between them. The order pad was readied in seconds. Hearts and stomachs were already set on what a table tent touted as the best seafood salad *à la Louis* served anywhere in Seattle—small wonder, considering the two-sixty-five pricetag.

Von's lofty claim lived up to all it promised. Mike had the crab variation, Roger the shrimp, and for the next twenty minutes they dived, without surfacing, into a pound of fresh seafood, crackling iceberg lettuce and slivered green pepper, quartered tomatoes not a day off the vine, two breakfasts' worth of hardboiled ranch eggs, a boodle of black *and* pimiento-stuffed Spanish olives, all topped with a house Thousand Island dressing backed with just enough chili sauce to make even a pair of ravenous teens pay attention.

"What're the lemon slices for?" Mike got around to asking only after he had pushed away his empty plate.

Roger shrugged at the saucerful of unsqueezed citrus in the middle of the table. "Maybe they thought we'd order ice tea."

"*Man*, I tell you ..." But there was no need to and Mike summed up his compliments to the chef by producing the Dutch Masters stogy imported from Ben Paris.

Both of them took their sweet time undressing the cigars, first fiddling with the paper bands, then alternately pinching and sniffing the pliant shafts of tobacco from stem to stern in an earnest effort to appear like they knew what they were doing. Actually, Roger had sampled a few segars in his callow youth: unendearing experimentation dating back to Leonard's short-lived career as a black marketeer in junior high school. Mike toyed with the personalized matches the Von's ashtray provided, but might never have got around to lighting up had it not been for their fussing waiter. His sure hand, guiding a Hotel Tropicana lighter, had the lads puffing like chimneys before he walked away with an order for after-dinner coffee.

Roger glanced at the server's back, then wrinkled his nose at the acrid taste invading his mouth. "I know this company sponsors his show, and all," he told his cigar, then Mike, critically, "but it still beats me why Ernie Kovacs smokes these lousy things."

"Edie Adams." Mike parked the big, brown butt in the ashtray and never touched it again.

The passing of the dinner hour had perked up foot traffic considerably. Purposeful pedestrians—couples, primarily—filled intersections and sidewalks and clogged up the heavy flow of cars attempting to turn. The older crowd headed for cross-street rivals the Blue Mouse and the Music Box. The younger set—among them punks who stopped outside the KNBX booth attached to the Warehouse of Music to flip off the on-the-air disc jockey—in the main gravitated toward the Coliseum.

A stylish lady of about fifty and her Leslie Hughes-attired husband had interrupted their march toward the 5th Avenue Theatre to window-shop at Rivkin's. It was when they crossed Pike with the light that she took notice of the youth near the corner they were approaching. Roger had stopped two feet short of the curb for an impromptu, but unsuccessful, attempt to blow smoke rings. A passing taxi honked its irritation and Mike hauled his friend onto the sidewalk by his elbow. The lads had decided on dessert and were headed east to do something about it.

"Look at that young man, will you," the bejeweled woman grumped. "Smoking a cheap cigar in public"—she swatted at the gray cloud following the object of her scorn—"when I'm certain he isn't any older than our William."

Her consort smiled at the chipper pair ahead of them. "What the devil, Doris? Those kids are having the time of their lives." He took her hand in his and pressed it.

The laughter didn't stop until Mike and Roger had reached the front door of the Home of the Green Apple Pie.

# *THE* SPORTING LIFE

It has long been a widely held belief in Seattle that, for more than sixty years, the city was bereft of national championship-caliber sports teams. For decades, this urban legend—perhaps an outgrowth of snobbery endemic to towns with big-league big heads—has been embraced by uninformed transplants, disgruntled fans and shortsighted sportswriters who should know better.

The story has it that the NBA Champion SuperSonics ended a title drought that began in 1917. That was the year Pete Muldoon's Seattle Metropolitans became the first American hockey franchise to win the Stanley Cup in the final series pitting the Mets against the temporarily not-so-immortal Montreal Canadiens. The fact is, the *real* drought appears to have begun with the Sonics whipping the Washington Bullets for the title on June 1, 1979. But for the consistency of the WNBA Storm and the University of Washington women's softball teams (with sporadic contributions by the football program), the thirst continues unslaked.

There were glimmerings of greatness as the midpoint of the Twentieth Century arrived: A young man born in Potlatch, Idaho, was getting set to pursue his dream of playing professional hockey. The owner of a local bread company had begun sponsoring a basketball team to compete in the Class AA city league. A heavy-hitting baseball Hall-of-Famer made a fateful career move that brought him to the boondocks. On small oval tracks like the Aurora Stadium Speedway, a California transplant started his climb to the big time at Indianapolis. A town once awash in football glory would eventually experience it again—but only after being treated to unexpected success by other collegiate athletic programs unaccustomed to the limelight.

Even now, looking back, the most clairvoyant fancier of sport can't be blamed for failing to have read the signs. Much like the dispirited Emerald City buff of 2012, the Queen City fan at the start of 1950 didn't have a lot of team pride to shout about. The Huskies had only a tie to show for four Rose Bowl appearances.* Basketball wasn't a staple yet. The Seattle Rainiers of the Pacific Coast League, the most popular minor-league team in the country, hadn't won a pennant since 1941. Boxing never seemed to have recovered since the town had screamed itself hoarse at the Al Hostak-Fred Steele title bout in 1938.** And apart from rowing, many in Seattle believed the only speedboat competition in the area took the form of mythic submarine races conducted offshore at Golden Gardens on Friday and Saturday nights.

Then something happened—a *lot* of somethings, as it turned out. Disparate ingredients began to come together and jell, ultimately earning local sportsmen a wealth of cups, pennants, purses, crowns and national titles (along with admirable near misses) that would have amazed the travel-weary producers of *Wide World of Sports*. As 1949 rolled into 1950, the city began to arise from the dust of an athletic wasteland to embark on the Golden Age of the Fifties. There would never be another decade like it in Seattle. Ever.

Like the beginning of life itself, it got under way in the water.

## 1950

Once attracting the largest crowds of any sport viewed in Seattle, collegiate rowing began gaining popularity all over again. Thousands of fans, new and seasoned, were drawn to the Montlake Cut that spring as they had been in the seminal years of Hiram Conibear and George Pocock way back in the Teens when the Huskies were called the Sun Dodgers. This campaign rewarded the faithful with the ultimate achievement in the eight-oar class. Meet after meet, Washington topped such traditional powers as Navy, Cornell and California to score a triple crown. Varsity, JV and Freshman crews each won the Intercollegiate Rowing Association (the other IRA)

---

* Against Navy in 1924, 14-all.

** Hostak, from Seattle, defeated Steele, of Tacoma, for the middle-weight championship at Civic Stadium before a crowd of 35,000—the largest to witness a boxing match in the city's history.

championship in their divisions, a feat to be unequaled by the program for nearly a half century.

But any residual cheering was drowned out just weeks later by a rumbling across Lake Washington.

The first most Seattleites knew of Stan Sayres' ambition to be the fastest man on water came midway in 1950. The owner of a Chrysler dealership in the Broadway District had already launched a series of speedy craft on which he painted the contradiction *Slo-Mo-Shun. Slo-Mos I* through *III* were fleet "limiteds" in the 225-cubic-inch engine class, capable of speeds of up to 80 mph. The auto retailer wanted to go faster. Up stepped a young Seattle boat designer named Ted Jones. Jones promised to deliver a world-record ride when Sayres ordered the fourth craft in the series, a larger "unlimited" hydroplane (U-27 to the American Powerboat Association). Anchor Jensen built the propeller-driven racer and they installed a sixteen-cylinder Allison aviation engine in the sleek hull.

On June 26, with Sayres at the wheel, the newest *Slo-Mo* topped 160 mph in a statute mile on the placid lake. The mark shattered the record Sir Malcolm Campbell had set in England in 1939.

Jones was a man of his word. After that, Sayres set his sights on Detroit, Michigan.

Back then, hydroplane racing was the sport of plutocrats. It was a close fraternity and upstarts weren't appreciated, especially those who couldn't trace their lineage to Grosse Pointe. Sayres wasn't daunted. Later in the summer of 1950, he brought the *Slo-Mo-Shun IV* to the Detroit River in pursuit of a piece of ornate hardware called the Gold Cup, the highest award offered by the sport. With Ted Jones driving, the *IV* proceeded to rewrite every record in the book on its way to humiliating once-formidable contenders like *My Sweetie* and *Miss Great Lakes.*

The Gold Cup was a fickle prize. Whoever won it could move the following year's race, named in its honor, to the sponsoring city. Sayres flew the Seattle Yacht Club burgee. This meant, in 1951, that competitors aligned with Detroit would have to make the long haul out west to retrieve what they viewed as their trophy. The stage was set for a rivalry that, true, wasn't yet nationwide in scope. But the battle for the Gold Cup would soon pit the two cities against one another with the kind of passionate antipathy previously reserved for the likes of Sparta and Athens.

Roostertail mania had come out of the henhouse.

## 1951

The initial Gold Cup regatta staged in Seattle would be only a time-out during that summer's furor over an entirely different sport. Seattle had long counted itself a baseball town and had been treated to quality players and coaching almost as soon as millionaire Emil Sick (father of Brew 66) bought the local franchise in 1937. He renamed the club the Rainiers, not for the mountain Seattle framed on a clear day but after his most popular beer, and built a 15,000-seat, state-of-the-art ballpark on (fittingly) Rainier Avenue and McClellan Street. From the onset, the Rs made themselves a potent force in the Pacific Coast League*, doing battle with yesteryear's Hollywood Stars, Portland Beavers, San Francisco Seals, Sacramento Solons, Oakland Oaks, along with the original Angels and Padres.

The Rainiers dominated the league in the years preceding World War II, winning consecutive pennants from 1939 to 1941 thanks to the pitching of the great Fred Hutchinson and the batting and basework of talents like Edo Vanni. But the war dispersed the star-studded roster, and the quality of coaching declined following the departure of manager Jack Lelivelt. Emil Sick, a man with deep pockets and a serious commitment to showcasing quality ball in Seattle, went shopping.

Rajah (Rogers) Hornsby was brought to town after years of managing elsewhere in the minor leagues. Though enshrined in the Hall of Fame in 1942 as a player, Hornsby found that his full twenty-two years in the majors had taught him just about everything there was to know about the game and how to instill it in those under his tutelage. The town crowded Garlic Gulch that summer to take in the batting of league MVP Jim Rivera (.352) and the pitching of twenty-game winner Marv Grissom. When it came to an end in the fall, Hornsby had fashioned a 99-68 season and a first-place finish for the

---

* There is a claim that, until the Dodgers and Giants moved west in 1958, the PCL was the third major baseball league in the country. A list of its quality players, and what they were paid to keep them out west, bear out at least part of this contention.

re-energized franchise.

But for a week that summer, the roar of packed houses at day games in Sicks' [sic] Stadium was challenged by a deeper, throatier racket just a mile due east. The unlimited hydros had come to town for the first time, and nobody knew quite what to make of it all. It was to be a crash course.

Brewer Emil Sick bought the financially strapped Seattle Indians in 1937 (a year before the above photo was taken). Local baseball fans were outraged when Sick renamed the PCL franchise the Rainiers. But three consecutive pennants (1939-1941) silenced complaints and by the time the Rainiers clinched championships in 1951 and '55, the Queen City was lapping up far more "Mountain Fresh" than any other brew on the local market. (PEMCO Webster & Stevens Collection, Museum of History & Industry, Seattle)

For sobering starters, the race would claim two lives. A boat hailing from Portland, the *Quicksilver*, would nose into a swell and take the driver, Orth Mathiot, and his mechanic, Ted Whittaker—

both belted into the two-seater—to their deaths in the third heat.[*] Bill O'Mara, who was calling the race live for KING-TV, knelt and led his unseen audience in the Lord's Prayer as the covering camera drifted heavenward. Viewers were transfixed and a sportscasting legend was born.

Although the feat was overshadowed by the tragedy, Stan Sayres' new speed demon, the *Slo-Mo-Shun V*, crushed the competition from Motor City and topped sister *IV*'s 1950 winning pace by some seven miles per hour. The Gold Cup would remain in Seattle and Detroit's vanquished would have to face yet another trip to Lake Washington in 1952 hoping to recoup lost honor. Vivid memories of the event would linger nearly as long as the town's original Queen City nickname.[**]

The 3-6-1 Husky football team deserves little mention but for the fact that it featured three All-Americans on an otherwise lackluster roster: defensive back Dick Sprague, quarterback Don (The Arm) Heinrich and fullback (Hustlin') Hugh McElhenny. Heinrich suffered a season-ending shoulder separation two weeks before the opener against Montana (which Washington did win, 58-7). Without The Arm's skill and leadership, however, the wheels quickly came off the wagon and The Dawgs, an appellation they would later earn, slunk to a seventh-place finish in the Pacific Coast Conference.

## 1952

Well-rounded fans—even those dejected by the woeful football season—were quickly cheered by an unusual athletic event held just three weeks into the new year.

In a day when unique barnstorming match-ups were yet to be kyboshed by the greed and inflexibility of iron-fisted athletic leagues and conferences, the Harlem Globetrotters crisscrossed the world playing colleges, AAU members and legitimate professional teams. Led by ball-handling deadeyes like six-four center Reece (Goose) Tatum and forward Louis (Babe) Pressley, Abe Saperstein's wizards of the hardwood took the game as seriously as the competition called for. As of January 20, 1952, the club's overall record stood at

---

[*] Seat belts, from then on, would be banned in the sport.

[**] After more than a century of use, it was shelved in 1982.

an astounding 3,999 wins to just 253 losses.*

Saperstein brought them to Seattle on January 21 confident of notching number 4,000. A small contingent from First Hill had a different idea.

Seattle University, nicknamed the Chieftains then, was just beginning to achieve prominence as an independent basketball power under coach Al Brightman. The coach had recruited the O'Brien twins, Johnny and Eddie, and concocted a potent fast-break style the Trotters probably hadn't bargained for when they agreed to appear in the Olympics fundraiser in Seattle that winter. The town went wild at the prospect of seeing the towering cagers from back east—so wild that the contest had to be moved from the pint-sized, on-campus SU gym to 12,500-seat Hec Edmundson Pavilion at the UofW. Every ducat sold was, if not owing to the opponents, then to see the great Louis Armstrong host the event.

The Globetrotters performed their renowned warm-up routine, bands played and actress Joan Caulfield, wearing a tight sweater, appeared on court to further whip up the packed house. But it wasn't long after the tip-off that Saperstein might well have considered changing the team's newly adopted theme, "Sweet Georgia Brown," to "I'll Never Smile Again." Five-foot-nine *center* John O'Brien unleashed a forty-three-point scoring barrage the Trotters were unable to defend or match. SU blew the lid off Hec Ed with an 84-81 victory that sent the men from Harlem out of town still one game shy of 4,000. Shaking his head after the loss, Goose Tatum (whose eighty-four-inch armspan had failed to smother the diminutive scoring machine while, himself, accounting for only twenty-three points) was heard to say of Johnny-O, "He's the playingest little man I ever did see."

The upset win was a plum for the Chieftain program, but only an *hors d'oeuvre* compared to the bigger and better things ahead in the Fifties for the Jesuit school.

The cheery mood carried over to spring and summer. Hopes were high for the defending-champion Rainiers, even though the club had lost manager Rogers Hornsby to the St. Louis Browns in the bigs

---

* This was the Globetrotter record cited by the local press in 1952. Since then, other sources have revised the win total downward to 3,571.

following his one, glorious season in town. But the Rs slipped to third in the PCL and stayed there. Fortunately, Seattle had other pompoms to shake.

In spite of its distance from Madison Square Garden main events—or, perhaps, because of it—Seattle had long been the Northwest's mecca for prizefighting. Quality boxers on par with Hostak and Steele kept local venues like the Arena and Eagles Auditorium bustling year-round and eventually attracted an Idaho native to Seattle via the Los Angeles fight scene. Famed manager and promoter Jack Hurley took middleweight Harry (Kid) Mathews under his wing in 1949 and over the course of the next two years steered his slugger through the best the area had to offer. In 1951, Hurley packed the beefed-up Kid off to New York City where, as a light heavy, he scored a number of impressive victories.

Hurley pulled strings and all but cast spells to boost Mathews into the heavyweight ranks and a title bout in July with champ Rocky Marciano at Yankee Stadium. Although The Rock ko'd the challenger in round two, *Seattle P-I* sports editor Royal Brougham had so hyped the fight that Mathews returned to a hero's welcome and an avid following in Seattle that made him a drawing card until the end of his 90*-7-6 career.

Days later, the town began gearing up for another battle of the thunderboats on the lake. Stan Sayres had ignited growing fan interest by piloting the *Slo-Mo IV* to a new world's speed record of 178 mph prior to the regatta. The handwriting was clearly posted on the wall for all comers. With Stan Dollar sitting in for Sayres, the *IV* was the only boat to finish the ninety-mile circuit (at a genteel 84 mph) in a less-calamitous race that did, nevertheless, see the *Such Crust IV* blow up, injuring driver Bill Cantrell.

Seattle was rapidly developing a taste for breakneck sport—and getting used to winning at it.

### 1953

Seattle University's triumph over the Globetrotters only temporarily shifted the limelight from the cross-town powerhouse Huskies. At the close of the 1952 season, Washington was ranked

---

* Sixty-one were by knockout.

sixth in the nation. Naturally, coach William Henry Harrison (Tippy) Dye was eyeing a second Pacific Coast Conference title. Sure enough, starters Mike McCutcheon, Chuck Koon, Doug McClary, Joe Cipriano and the man who made the hook shot an almost indefensible weapon, Bob Houbregs, handed their mentor a 15-1 conference record and the championship. Looking ahead, local aficionados began wondering aloud who was good enough to deny the Huskies the NCAA crown. As the luck of the draw would have it, Al Brightman and the O'Brien brothers were provided with a chance to have a say in the matter.

Seattle U and Washington didn't meet during the regular season, and every Queen City citizen with a pulse had an opinion about which had the best five. The Chieftains were admitted to the twenty-two-team Big Dance without a conference affiliation and reached the Sweet Sixteen in Corvallis after a convincing win over Wyoming (80-64). The Huskies humbled LSU in the first round, 88-69, and advanced to the same bracket. Against Seattle University.

Frenzied fans were on tenterhooks as the newspapers printed extra editions to cover every angle of the contest, and local bookies worked overtime posting wagers on the "dream game"—a dream, yes, for Washington, but as it turned out a bona fide nightmare for SU. Chieftain pennants flew at half-staff on the hill the day following the 92-70 drubbing in Oregon.

Washington went on to survive the Elite Eight round by outpointing Santa Clara 74-62. For the only time in the program's history, the Huskies reached the Final Four. The occasion was not a happy one for Dye's team, however, who were handed their lunch in Kansas-made buckets that totaled 79 points to a meager 53[*]. Still, the hoopsters from Hec Ed—most of them graduating seniors—could deservedly revel in the season's third-place ranking nationally.

The Sweet Sixteen battering was a bitter pill for the Chieftains to swallow. But history would note that the basketball fortunes of the two schools hit extremes in success and failure at the tournament, and then reversed themselves. Tippy Dye would never floor a team as dominant as '53's Varsity five. On the other hand, while Al Brightman would lose the All-American "Gold Dust Twins" to

---

[*] The Jayhawks went on to lose to Indiana in the nail-biting final, 68-69.

graduation and pro baseball careers (and himself depart following the 1956 season), the ambitious program was within a couple of years of building a team that would make most fans forget about the shellacking in Corvallis.

The mettle of burgeoning numbers of hydro fanatics was put to a test when *Slo-Mo-Shun V* was damaged, and ultimately sank, during a pre-race test run with Lou Fageol at the wheel. The forces of darkness from Detroit may well have viewed the setback as their opportunity to recapture glory from the pests on Puget Sound. But Stan Sayres, ever the innovator and tactician, turned misfortune into gold for yet a fourth time. He divided driving duties between the best talent on Lake Washington. Fageol piloted the *Slo-Mo IV* to victory in the second heat, while Joe Taggart outran the pack in the first and third stanzas. Records fell again and the Detroit Yacht Club's trophy case went empty for another year.

The win left the lake boiling.

## 1954

It almost escaped notice that local athletes failed to excel on gridirons, hardwood courts, in the city's rings and along the Montlake Cut in '54. It was the Year of the Thunderboats.

Greater Seattle's prepubescent boys fashioned crude hydroplane models from scrap wood and, behind Raleigh and J.C. Higgins bikes, dragged them around every school playground and parking lot in town. Premier kiddie-show host Stan Boreson named his lethargic basset hound sidekick No Mo Shun. During the first week in August, exasperated employers rented television sets so that antsy workers could stay abreast of the time trials at the office instead of calling in sick. Beating the world's car capital at a speed sport had become, if not bewitchment, then a condition verging on mass obsession. Emmett Watson wrote of the phenomenon, "The country had changed and Seattle had changed with it. People became enamored of speed and noise. They turned out in great throngs to watch the belching, roaring hydroplanes...."* *Throngs* is an accurate description of the numbers drawn to Lake Washington during Seafair. A quarter of a million—*half* the city's population—squeezed into every available

---

* From *Once Upon a Time in Seattle*, Lesser Seattle Publishing, 1992 (pg. 112).

vantage point to get a glimpse of the streaking mahogany hulls that year.

At the end of the day, the Sayres camp had worked its wonder yet again. Powered by a beefier, but chancy, Rolls-Merlin engine, the resurrected *Slo-Mo-Shun V* upped the bar on its Allison-driven competition. Although Detroit's *Miss U.S. II* scored a second-place finish, Lou Fageol and the *Slo-Mo V* outclassed every entry (including older sister *IV*, still Allison-equipped) to astonish the sport with a blistering 99 mph average speed for the race.

Not all Motown skippers came away empty-handed, however. (Now *Wild*) Bill Cantrell had a cold martini delivered to his right mitt after his steering-challenged *Gale IV* left the racecourse in the second heat, hopped a bulkhead and landed in the middle of Dr. F.A. Black's Gold Cup garden party near the Floating Bridge. The wirephoto of Cantrell toasting his host from a seat atop the *Gale's* engine cowling was reprinted on sports pages across the country—with the possible exception of those in Detroit.

## 1955

Royal Brougham dubbed it "the greatest pulse-pumping, eye-popping pennant race in Seattle baseball history." Your Old Neighbor would have been the one to know. He had been the *P-I's* sports editor since 1920. Movie critic William Arnold later recalled, "The 1955 season was the most magical of all Rainier seasons … and veterans of that summer claim Seattle had never been so caught up in anything, before or since."* Given the lengthy time frame of the dramatic doings, the assertion may well have been true.

But, first, a word about another motor sport.

Years before speed junkies fixated on the unlimited hydros, the town had been a hotbed of auto racing. North Seattle was home to four major tracks, at one time or another, that dotted the Highway 99 corridor all the way out to the King-Snohomish county line at 205th. The quarter-mile ovals were ideally suited to stock cars, jalopies and, especially, midget racers. By war's end, when the sport was revived, tracks like the one adjacent to Playland Amusement Park attracted

---

* From William Arnold's video review appearing August 23, 1999, in the *Seattle Post-Intelligencer.*

large crowds lured by fierce competition and the gutty snarl of blown Offenhauser engines.

In 1945, a crack mechanic named Clark (Shorty) Templeman slipped behind the wheel and kicked off an ever-expanding career across the Northwest and, eventually, the entire nation. Having acquired journeyman's experience as he tallied five Washington State midget racing championships (and three more in Oregon), Templeman made the quantum leap from the short tracks to the big time at the Brickyard in Indianapolis. His first ride there came in 1955, starting thirty-first, in a race remembered not for its winner, Bob Sweikert, but for the death of two-time victor Bill Vukovich on the fifty-sixth lap.

There was no television coverage of the 500 back when, so Seattle had its ear pressed to speakers citywide that Memorial Day as Sid Collins and his crew called the race wire-to-wire over the Indianapolis Motor Speedway Radio Network. Templeman bowed out on lap 142 owing to transmission trouble, but still recorded a respectable eighteenth place, considering.

Diminutive in stature though he was, Shorty Templeman had begun acquiring a sizable reputation among devotees of *fast*.

By July it was becoming evident that the also-ran Rainiers of recent years were pulling together to make a serious run for the pennant. During the off-season, GM Dewey Soriano had persuaded his friend Fred Hutchinson to return home to manage the team that had been his springboard to the majors. As an inducement, Hutch was given *carte blanche* to reorganize the clubhouse however he saw fit. He accepted the guarantee and ran with it, making over eighty personnel changes before the end of the spring. From that point on, it was a battle royal among the Rainiers, Padres, Stars and the hated Angels for the PCL top spot.

However, the civic adrenalin rush wasn't confined to Sicks' Stadium that summer.

The week of qualifying for the Gold Cup race on August 7 found grim, foreboding winds blowing in the direction of the Seattle camp. A sudden gust of it destroyed the defending champion *Slo-Mo-Shun V*. Tens of thousands of television viewers watched in horror as the U-37 performed a near-perfect flip in the backstretch at 165 mph, seriously injuring driver Lou Fageol. The shattered hydroplane would never again compete under the fabled *Slo-Mo* name.

Detroit came to Seattle with new resolve and a plan to back it. Still, fresh blood was there to greet the *Gale* boats, the *U.S., Miss Cadillac* and the wallowing five-ton, twin-engined *Such Crust III*. A brash young limited driver named Bill Muncey had stepped up to the big boats in a brand-new, state-of-the-art firecracker called the *Miss Thriftway*, designed by Ted Jones. While Muncey ran away from most of the competition (even Joe Taggart in the *Slo-Mo IV* blew an engine trying to catch him), the *Such Crust* was used as an effective, wake-churning blocker that slowed the *Thriftway* just enough to give the *Gale V* a faster average speed over the full ninety miles—without winning a single heat.* Under established rules, the *Gale* was awarded a 400-point bonus for outhustling the *Thriftway* by some 4.53 seconds. Unaware of this twist, jubilant fans left for home and Channel 4 returned to regular programming in the belief that Muncey's 1,025-point total for two firsts and one third-place finish had kept the Gold Cup in Seattle for another year. Not so. A savvier Channel 5 crew stood by live until the decree was handed down making Lee Schoenith's *Gale V*, with 1,225 points, the actual winner of the regatta.

Seattle hydro fans went ballistic, local boosters cried foul in the press, boycotts of the Cadillac and Chevrolet brands were called for, and the Detroit boats had to be quietly trucked out of town to escape vandalism. But the Motor City entry had won fair and square under reigning statutes, and THE cup—*Seattle's* cup—slipped away after a five-year lock by the city that had come to call the trophy its own.

Fortunately, Fred Hutchinson's intrepid Rainiers were there to apply the balm necessary to help heal this gaping wound to civic pride. Sicks' Stadium, along with the freeloaders' perch to the east called Tightwad Hill, began to fill for every game. It was nearly impossible to walk down any residential street in town on warm August and September evenings that summer without hearing Leo Lassen's rivety call of every pitch and hit through open windows to

---

* In fairness, test pilot Alvin (Tex) Johnston's unscripted barrel rolls over the lake in a Boeing 707 prototype likely gave the huge crowd a bigger rush than anything that happened on the racecourse.

radioland.

Hutch did work magic that season. Without a single twenty-game winner or hitter batting over .300, he simply outcoached the next-best during a campaign that had even lukewarm baseball fans on their feet. His club took the pennant with a 95-77 record, three games ahead of San Diego in a race that went down to the wire and jangled nerve endings from Vancouver to Vancouver.

The spotlight still shown brightly on the Queen City as the year drew to a close.

## 1956

The main thing about the Seattle fan base then was that, with such a smorgasbord of heartily embraced sports and events to choose from, he or she seldom wanted for a winner. Though heavy hearted in the knowledge that 1955 had marked the end of the *Slo-Mo* era—and doubtless troubled by the departure of Fred Hutchinson to manage the Cincinnati Reds the next season—life went on and hope sprang eternal for local athletes and the people who promoted them.

The extent or longevity of acceptance by no means limited the variety of sport available to the enthusiastic town. Wrestling—before roaring back on television in the Fifties as "Rasslin'"—had enjoyed sporadic bouts of popularity dating back to early in the century and the days of B.F. (Doc) Roller's flamboyant career in the ring. (Queen) Helene Madison—winner of three gold medals in the 1932 Los Angeles Olympics—inspired not only a legion of rooters, but a generation of hometown girls to test the waters of competitive swimming. Herman Brix (briefly Tarzan in the 1930s) helped make track and field a headline grabber on local sports pages. The wild-and-woolly Sammamish Slough Race for a time became an annual boat buster attracting thousands. Golf, horse racing, drag racing, semi-pro football, marathon dancing—each had a distinct place on the motley menu of a city that thrived on sports as much as it did on its vaunted fresh air and clean water.

A notable discovery of the Fifties was that Seattle continued to produce some outstanding basketball teams in an age when the NBA had little currency with fans. Furthermore, by mid-decade, it was no longer a secret that not all the great roundball was being played at

Hec Ed or on the SU campus.

George Buchan was baking Seattle's favorite mass-produced bread by 1948 when he was persuaded to sponsor a team initially competing in the city's amateur basketball league. Nationwide, a growing number of companies—some of them large corporations—had begun bankrolling highly visible athletic squads as a form of effective advertising. Employment was a perk frequently offered talented recruits in a time when living-wage professional contracts were few and far between. A basketball sponsorship was especially desirable because of limited team size and minimal expenditures for equipment and uniforms.

The Buchan Bakers undoubtedly helped their benefactor sell more bread. They immediately dominated the city league and, in the early Fifties, boosted their profile by joining the Amateur Athletic Union. The AAU was the playground for a number of nationally known teams sponsored by the likes of Caterpillar, Phillips Petroleum and Goodyear Tire and Rubber. Bolstered by the addition of ex-Huskies Cipriano, McClary, Koon and McCutcheon, the Bakers found they could hold their weight against most rivals over the thirty-game season. But the team's disappointing exits from the 1952 and '54 national tournaments made it clear that the club was still a few octane short of being able to run with the established powerhouses. General Manager Warren Howard hired a new coach and, for the 1955-56 campaign, brought on board George Swyers from West Virginia Tech, six-five guard Stan Glowaski from Seattle University, along with Husky Dean Parsons, a six-foot-eight forward. Six-nine center Bruno Boin, a sophomore letterman from the UofW, joined them for the national tourney.

The Bakers reached the finals in Denver and easily dispatched the first trio of opponents, thanks in part to Boin's deadly hook shots. But the streak left them facing a foe of goliathan proportions, the Phillips Oilers. Even the most stalwart among the growing body of Seattle fans didn't give the doughboys much of a chance. The Oklahomans had clinched nine AAU titles since 1940, including the previous year's championship. From the onset, it looked as if the Bakers would hand the oilmen the tenth on a golden platter.

OFFICIAL
PROGRAM

Price

**25¢**

N? 3018

**49th National A.A.U.
Basketball Championship
Of America**

**Denver Auditorium
Annex**

**March 19-24, 1956**

*Under the Auspices of the
Rocky Mountain Association
of A. A. U. of the United States*

Buchan's Bakers
vs.
Peoria Cats
brought to you by the bakers of
*Buchan's*
the bonnie-good bread

Seattle's Buchan Baking Company, once the largest independently owned bakery on the West Coast, began sponsoring post-collegiate basketball in 1948. In 1956, the Bakers defeated a heavily favored Phillips 66 team to bring home the city's first national basketball championship. The Seattle SuperSonics would duplicate the feat 23 years later. (Alec Buchan Collection)

Trailing 23-12 early on, the Seattleites scrapped back to take a 31-30 lead at halftime. Phillips tied the game 57-all with two minutes remaining. In a spectacular Hail Mary that filled every breadbox in the region with Buchan tartan wrappers, Swyers nixed the odds of winning in overtime, drove the lane to the foul line and fired a one-handed shot off the backboard that split the net with no time left.

The 59-57 decision went a long way to whetting the local appetite for white bread and many more servings of basketball.

Elsewhere on the local sports front, the Husky Junior Varsity eight won the IRA crown again, and Clark Templeman began conquering tracks all over the country on his way to earning the first-ever National Midget Car Racing Association championship.

Of course, it was the effort to retrieve the purloined Gold Cup that summoned the largest television audience in the city's history to that time. But getting the trophy back from Detroit would prove even more contentious than the previous year's tussle. To be sure, there was no question that the red-hot *Miss Thriftway* had bested all competition with relative ease. After the race ended, however, judges ruled that Bill Muncey had destroyed a buoy on the seventh lap of the final heat. The *Thriftway* was disqualified and the *Miss Pepsi* declared the winner. A legal battle ensued during which Channel 5, having covered the Detroit race over the entire ABC Network, came forward with film proving that Muncey had not touched the marker as he skimmed past it. The decision was reversed and, this time, it was the Seattle gang that fled town with the prize.

Sadly, a devastating preface to the regatta, and the heart-breaking consequence of it, dampened the celebration back home. *Slo-Mo IV*—Stan Sayres' "old lady"—was destroyed during a pre-race test run on the Detroit River. The man who had brought hydromania to Seattle was unable to bring himself to view the wreckage, unlike tens of thousands of citizens for what would be the closest thing to a state funeral ever held in the city.[*]

Stanley M. Sayres died of a heart attack a month later.

## 1957

Seattle's fascination with water sports was temporarily diverted by the frozen variety in late 1956. By the turn of the year, the city's Western Hockey League franchise, the Americans, was renewing interest in a sport that had been on the wane since the disbanding of

---

[*] An elevated walkway built for viewing the splintered hull was erected behind KING-TV's Aurora Avenue studio. Parking started a mile away.

the Metropolitans in 1924.

Professional hockey on the coast showed signs of a rebirth after World War II. At first, its success locally was as shaky as the young league in charge. Both organizations changed names—the PCHL became the Western Hockey League in 1952 and Seattle went from being known as the Ironmen to the Bombers. Then the stumbling franchise folded for a season because of poor attendance. The club was salvaged under the new name, Americans, just in time to sign a young center who had begun his career in the Canadian junior leagues. The sensational new recruit brought them back to the Ice Arena in droves.

(Golden) Guyle Fielder wowed everybody that year by breaking the professional single-season scoring record with 122 points (goals plus assists) on his way to becoming the league's MVP, the first of four consecutive selections. With teammates Val Fonteyne (the least-penalized player of all time) and Charlie Hodge (future Vezina-award winner for the best NHL goalie), the Americans skated to first place in the WHL that season. Hockey was back.

So was Shorty Templeman in the midgets, on his way to a second straight national racing title.

The Gold Cup regatta came home to new digs that August. The classy Stan Sayres Memorial Park, built with the help of donations provided by thousands of fans, included the nation's first permanent pit facility for the unlimiteds. The fiftieth run for the trophy attracted a record field of twenty hopefuls (three of them from California). The Detroit entries might just as well have not shown up for the event as the first three places were nailed down convincingly by thunderboats flying the flag of the Seattle Yacht Club. The *Miss Thriftway* became the first unlimited to crack the 100-mph average-speed barrier over a 90-mile Gold Cup course (its historic 101.7 mark earning Muncey the coveted 400 bonus points that had snatched victory from his camp in 1955). Second and third spots were captured by Arizona millionaire Bill Waggoner's *Shanty I* and *Maverick* tandem.

The win sent a clear message, should it have been needed, that the Muncey era was under way.

Mira Slovak, the Flying Czech, puts on a game face as the Wahoo is readied for qualifying for the 1957 Gold Cup race on Lake Washington. The U-77 finished in a tie for seventh at the 50th running of The Cup. The Miss Thriftway, Shanty I and Maverick placed one, two and three respectively. (M. Barrett photo)

Two weeks later that same August, a mad rush for tickets to Sicks' Stadium commenced. Only, the wads of cash being traded for pricey ($10-$15-$20) pasteboard weren't buying box-seat admissions to see the sagging Rainiers.

Thomas (Pete) Rademacher was born in tiny Tieton, in Eastern Washington. He came to Seattle as a young adult and became a favorite fighting in a series of boxing tournaments and Golden Gloves competitions. In 1953, he won the U.S. Amateur Heavyweight Championship, beating Zora Folley in the process, and secured an All-Army title three years later. In 1956, he qualified for the Olympic Games in Melbourne where he belted his way to a gold medal. It was his last hurrah as an amateur heavyweight, a career he closed out with a 72-7 win-loss record.

After planting his feet on American soil once again, Rademacher boldly announced that he intended to launch the professional phase of his career by challenging the best there was—namely, world heavyweight champ Floyd Patterson. It marked the only time a fighter making his professional debut had dropped the gauntlet on a reigning champion. It was a preposterous pairing, of course, and probably wouldn't have come off outside of Rademacher's adopted hometown. Somehow, promoters quickly came up with the $250,000 guarantee Patterson's people demanded and the fight was set for August 22, two days after Rademacher's twenty-ninth birthday.

Rademacher landed a lucky punch in the second to drop the champion. But only fleetingly. Patterson quickly recovered to pummel the challenger from the third round on, decking him a half-dozen times before putting out the amateur's lights with a KO in the sixth.

The bout was to go down as a curious—if not farcical—footnote in the annals of modern prizefighting. It also served as a valuable lesson to locals in how to more wisely spend their sports dollars.

North of the Canal, the University of Washington introduced its fourth head football coach in six years. The young ex-Sooner's inaugural season was far from inspiring: 3-6-1 (sixth place in the PCC). Much better things lay ahead for Jim Owens, however.

Meanwhile, Seattle fans had only a matter of months in which to compose themselves before becoming swept up by events in the stellar year just around the corner.

## 1958

Roger's mother was in California that March, attending to her ailing father. The eighth-grader and his dad bached well together. In the absence of the chief cook, they got by on Van Camp's pork and beans and the Swanson frozen TV dinners that were all the rage then. They thrived on the diet: Roger continued to grow alarmingly and his dad failed to shed an ounce.

Both were sports fans, avid followers of the hydroplane wars (Roger had scars on his black Schwinn's fenders to prove it), and totally devoted to Gillette's Friday Night Fights broadcasts (lightheavy Archie Moore was a household hero). And they were just beginning to cultivate an interest in the NFL games that were finally reaching this remote region on television.

But the elder was the lone, *true* basketball fanatic at home. Neither of his sons had shown much ability, or interest, in the game he had excelled at in high school and college until a flag forced him to get serious and spend more time on his stud spectator now, he had been fired up about the success of t Bakers in 1956. During the past year, he had found himself scour the sports pages of both dailies to drink in all the news there was about the once-again ascending Seattle University Chieftains. And there had been plenty.

SU's second-year coach, John Castellani, had assembled another fine team. Francis Saunders, Don Ogorek, Jerry Frizzell, Jim Harney and (Sweet) Charlie Brown, an Indiana transfer, would have been a terrific starting line-up for just about any school. But Castellani iced the cake with the addition of six-six swingman Elgin Baylor. The move steered the Chieftain program in the direction of greatness. Seattle U reached the NIT quarterfinals at the end of Castellani's first season, and Baylor topped off his sophomore year as the nation's leading rebounder and third-best scorer (29.7 ppg). Anybody could see these stats were just a happy harbinger of things to come.

SU was invited to the twenty-four-team March mania marathon in '58. In the West Regionals, the Chiefs whipped Wyoming, squeaked by San Francisco State and topped California to close out the round. Could it get any better? Roger's dad wondered after digesting all that Boyd Smith, the *P-I* sportswriter, had to say about it all. Absolutely, both of them learned.

SU wound up facing tourney favorite Kansas State the following Friday night in the tip-off to Final Four action. Implausible as it seems now, as it did then, the game wasn't even a fair fight. Before the largest crowd ever to see an NCAA tournament game, Elg and Sweet Charlie dominated the boards so effectively that the overwhelmed Wildcats went for nearly ten minutes in the second half without scoring a point. It didn't matter, really, because Seattle U had already put away a game whose outcome the loftiest prayers of the Jesuit faithful could not have anticipated: 73-51.

The shocker put SU on a rung no other collegiate basketball team from the city had ever reached—or ever would again.

Never mind that the final would pit the Chieftains against Kentucky in its own backyard, Louisville (where the integrated Seattle team would receive less-than-lukewarm support from the ite fans in attendance). Never mind that Kentucky's legendary headman, Adolph Rupp, had coached more than 600 games to Castellani's sixty. Never mind that Elgin Baylor had sustained a broken rib during the Kansas State victory the night before. Never mind the odds. Never mind anything else. KING-TV's Bill O'Mara was in Louisville and the whole outrageous improbability would be there on Channel 5 Saturday night at 7:00 P.M. in dazzling black and white.

Roger's dad got up that morning sparring with the nervous fidgets that had poked at him decades earlier before big games with Yakima and Toppenish. So he filled the a.m. hours with a diverting stem-to-stern housecleaning in preparation for the possible return of his wife the following week. Stores of Nalley chili and Sunny Jim essentials were running low, calling for a trip to the Safeway on Eastlake later on. And as long as that would take the Plymouth wagon so close to town, it seemed like an excellent idea to push on for Warshal's Sporting Goods to have a look at the newest in Coleman camping gear. He and his son failed to make it that far south in the downtown core.

Distracted by the Embassy Theatre's Third Avenue marquee, the driver found a parking spot across from MacDougall's department store on Second. The lure of a Joel McCrea triple feature was too much for them to turn down on a drizzly Saturday afternoon, especially with hours to kill before the whopper game of the year. They caught most of *Wichita* and enjoyed *Black Horse Canyon* so much they hung around for the last course, *Trooper Hook*. The rest of the day just slipped away, as so often happened then in a cheap, comfortable seat furnished by a low-end movie house that didn't time its patrons.

It was nearly a quarter-till-six, and sunny, when they stumbled from the Embassy's Union Street entrance realizing that time was wasting. The father had a rumble in his stomach and a bee in his bonnet as they reached the end of the block and turned north. During one of the McCrea epics, he had made up his mind that the significance of this Saturday night called for more than the usual frozen-chicken-pot-pie fare; that Seattle U playing for all the money, marbles and chalk clamored for something *special*.

So they lit out for the Pike Place Market moments before the elder guessed the pungent provisioner was set to close. Only, the people's grocer didn't seem to have a pulse left, judging from the lack of activity to be seen once they were five steps inside. When they thought about it, there hadn't been three pedestrians to dodge in the three blocks they had covered in as many minutes. And maybe only two cars along their route. Saturday was the night Seattle traditionally whooped it up in grand style. But here it was coming up on the dinner hour and the town seemed deader than the proverbial doornail. The Market was all but deserted, too, and Roger's dad set out for the only seafood stall that still had its overhead lights on. There, they found a tall, tubercular-looking man shoveling slushy, shaved ice out into the gutter running along the edge of Pike Place.

"Sure I got 'em," the man said having stopped shoveling to answer the inquiry around a drooping Camel. "Sold a lot today—only about two, three pounds left. Best cooked peelers around."

They closed the deal quickly—a dollar-fifty for the lot—and the fishmonger deftly captured his remaining shrimp stock in white, waxed paper, taped it, bagged it and taped that, too.

"You got under an hour," the vendor warned them after a quick look at his watch.

Roger's dad waved back his understanding.

The man stuffed the money in a paper sack holding his day's receipts and turned out the lights.

They clipped north as far as the Athenian and persuaded the owner to sell them a bag of putts ten seconds after he had turned the OPEN side of the door sign to CLOSED. Then the two of them were outside on Pike Place, jogging down the middle of the narrow street that hadn't seen a moving car in ten minutes.

The father knew the city as well as any cabby and probably would have cleaned up on fares owing to the scarcity of taxis that evening. In fact, the only bus they saw, incoming on Westlake, was empty and traveling at a high rate of speed in the general direction of Bob Murray's Dog House. Uncharacteristically, the parent role model ran a yellow light crossing Denny and slowed only for a rolling California stop turning right against a red signal onto Valley Street.

The Plymouth's automatic transmission allowed Roger's dad a

free right hand that he used to begin looting the bag of doughnut balls from the paper sack between them. By the time they skimmed across the metal grating on the University Bridge, both had powdered-sugar goatees and white streamers striping their coat fronts. Roger stopped chewing while they waited for a green light northbound on Roosevelt Way at Forty-fifth. The intersection was the crossroads of northeast Seattle and it was still light enough to see that a baseball, thrown in any direction, wouldn't have hit a pedestrian nor a vehicle. There simply weren't any. Everyone had holed up in front of their own or somebody else's television set; that failing, they had glued themselves to a radio to hear Rod Belcher call the game on KOL. The town's watering holes seemed to be the only public places bringing out the living, as witnessed by the overflowing Duchess Tavern where it looked, as they passed, as if more than a hundred people had wedged themselves in before the booming twenty-one-inch set above the bar.

"God, I hope those kids can pull it off tonight." The edgy benediction was delivered just as the Plymouth scuffed tires pulling up to the curb. Headlights and ignition were shut off, although the key was left in place, and the driver joined his lanky son in a dash for the unlocked front door of their Bryant-district home. Roger warmed up the Motorola and adjusted the rabbit ears while his dad, manning the kitchen, dumped the shrimp in a casserole dish and quickly concocted an ersatz cocktail sauce from catsup and Tabasco that neither of them touched. They shared the feast set before them on a TV tray in front of the living-room davenport. By the time the tip-off came, each of them had established his own rote method of cleaning, disposing of tails and shells and gobbling the sweet, inch-and-a-half-long crustaceans.

The Chieftains fought the good fight. They were still in the lead with seven minutes left in the game, 60-58. But Baylor, hampered by his painful injury and hamstrung by four fouls throughout most of the second half, wasn't enjoying his best performance in the tournament that, anyway, would ultimately make him its most valuable player. Frizzell and Brown picked up most of the work around the boards. But when Sweet Charlie and Don Ogorek fouled out, SU's tank—running on fumes—hit empty. The wily Rupp exploited every Chieftain shortcoming and the contest was over well before the eventual 72-84 count.

After the game ended, Roger's dad tuned in the last few minutes of *Gunsmoke* on Channel 7. Then it was back to KING for the *Lawrence Welk Show*, a choice that made doing homework on a Saturday night seem strangely appealing to Roger. His father wished him a glum "sleep well" around 11:00 and went off to bed to bury dashed hopes under nine hours of shuteye. Roger yawned himself into putting aside his American history text a half hour later. Neither of them had remembered to dispose of the pile of soggy shrimp husks on the drainboard, and they awoke in the morning to a kitchen that smelled like an empty salmon trawler under a hot July sun. Roger elected to use his mother's make-do incense substitute in dealing with the obnoxious odor: lighting a length of twine and allowing it to smolder harmlessly over the sink.

Their governess arrived home the following Tuesday. The kitchen still smelled of rotting sea life and burnt string. And Roger's dad remained as bitterly disappointed in the Chieftains' loss as he would have been had the Confederacy won the Civil War. Most of Seattle felt the same way.

Clark Templeman was there on Memorial Day to briefly rev up the pokey local pulse. On his way to a third-consecutive national midget racing championship, he had stopped off at Indianapolis for a second shot at the 500 trophy. He and his KurtisKraft-Offenhauser survived the fatal six-car smashup on the first lap. But Templeman had used a lot of lining avoiding it and was forced to retire with spent brakes after 116 circuits, finishing nineteenth. If there was a bright spot, it was that he was running only one mile per hour off Jimmy Bryan's pace of 144 mph. And Templeman would return.

Few victories in Seattle sports history are as inspiring as the Washington eight-man crew's gold medal finish at the Berlin Olympics in 1936. Although not as renowned as Jess Owens' quadruple gold-bashing of the myth of Aryan physical superiority, the Husky lump-in-the-throat, come-from-behind triumph over supremely confident German and Italian crews rates a lofty place in the pantheon of righteous athletic feats.

Incredibly, yet another achievement of this stature occurred on July 19, 1958. At the time, the Soviet Union and the United States were locked in the Cold War, a bitter, no-guns struggle for world domination. In spite of the ongoing rift, both governments temporarily put aside hard feelings to promote a "people-to-people" rowing competition on the Khimki Reservoir in Moscow. It was to be the six best entries the USSR could bring to the race versus the only crew invited from America—from *any*where: the University of Washington Varsity eight. Al Ulbrickson, who had coached the celebrated Husky shell in Berlin, was well versed in the challenges, and the ramifications, of an international meet. It wasn't enough that the Soviets were already leading the embryonic space race after the launch of Sputnik the previous summer. Now, they were stacking the deck for a public-relations coup by having the Seattleites face the dreaded Trud Club from Leningrad. Weeks earlier, Trud had left everyone—including Washington—in its wake at the Henley Regatta on the Thames. The formidable Soviet crew was hungering for still more glory. But Ulbrickson had had time since Henley to carefully evaluate the foe.

It shaped up to be the kind of engagement that Seattle supporters hoped would inspire at least a "respectable" showing from the hometown contingent. And with that faith, KOMO sent a young local sportscaster named Keith Jackson to Moscow to call the race live on radio from eleven time zones away.

Houselights all over the Queen City popped on during the wee hours of the 19th, timed to the opening of the scratchy broadcast. At the onset, Trud and a Soviet Army crew inched out into the lead on a choppy, wind-blown course Husky stroke John Sayre described as "just like Lake Washington." The UofW shell, the *Swiftsure*, responded accordingly. Upping the stroke to thirty-four, the Huskies closed the gap. Trud was their only competition now. By the midway point, 1,000 meters, the *Swiftsure* had forged ahead of Leningrad by a half length. The pace never moderated. At the finish line, Washington was in open water—a win of more than a length over the previous world-beaters.

Even the Soviet crowd ringing the reservoir gave the Americans a standing ovation. Keith Jackson was hoarse, but his obvious elation was unmistakable over the patchwork of long-distance connections. Back home, the police received several calls from the uninformed complaining of noisy, middle-of-the-night jubilation at certain brightly lit homes in normally quiet neighborhoods. Roger's dad went back to bed, grinning, by the dawn's early light.

If the waters of Khimki Reservoir proved inhospitable to some, then Lake Washington was a flat-out beast to nearly all of the participants in the 1958 Gold Cup Regatta. They represented yacht clubs from all over North America now, not just Seattle and Detroit: Lake Mead, Buffalo, Windmill Pointe, Lake Tahoe, Spokane and the Royal Canadian. But pedigree didn't matter a whit in this race. Of the sixteen unlimiteds that qualified for the event, a dozen weren't around at the end of the final heat, let alone able to answer the bell to get in it.

Bill Muncey's exit was by far the most dramatic, via the accident that is still recalled in hushed voices whenever the hydros race. The *Thriftway* lost its rudder traveling at 145 mph just after crossing the starting line. As the wayward rocket bore down on a boomful of spectator craft, a Coast Guard cutter chanced to cross its path and intercept the wrath of the 6,600-pound U-60. Broadside. The steel forty-footer sank with the *Thriftway* imbedded in its hull before rescuers arrived. An estimated 500,000 onlookers gasped as one as the wreckage slipped beneath the waves leaving Muncey and Coast Guard crew bobbing in the chop, somehow—remarkably—barely the worse for wear.

The balance of the carnage was largely mechanical in nature— twisted quill shafts, damaged props, blown superchargers and other maladies common to the classic three-pointers. The Cantrell-driven *Gale V* was the only Detroit entry to place in the top five, finishing third behind *Coral Reef*, running out of Tacoma. With the *Thriftway* no longer a factor, a new icon emerged from the Stan Sayres pits that day: the U-8 *Hawaii Kai III* with Jack Regas at the wheel. Industrialist Edgar Kaiser had deeded over the tropical-rose-and-coral-colored unlimited to the crew who had fine-tuned the *Slo-Mos IV* and *V* to glory. Their unmatched skill culminated in shepherding the *Kai* to a perfect 2,000-point performance at record speeds.

This Gold Cup win was the definitive statement about Seattle being a one-boat town—or not. If any had wondered.

## 1959

The past August's palpitations carried over to the beginning of the hockey season in the fall. Seattle's WHL franchise had changed its name to the Totems for the 1958-59 season, a brand it would carry for the next seventeen years as its reputation spread and local support grew stronger.

Future National Hockey League manager Keith Allen guided the Totems to a 40-27-3 record that saw them average nearly four goals per game. Rudy Filion and Guyle Fielder, now well on his way to amassing the second-highest career point total in professional hockey's history (behind only Wayne Gretzky), prevailed over tough opponents that included the ever-ornery Portland Buckaroos (extra security was always on hand for their memorable tilts in the Arena). The Totems ran away with the Western Hockey League title that inaugural year in what, given hindsight, may have been the club's finest campaign.

Then an unaccustomed dry spell set in during the spring and summer. John Castellani had resigned from Seattle University within weeks of his team's exceptional showing in Louisville. A recruiting violation resting squarely on the shoulders of the coach rocked the school, and Elgin Baylor's decision not to return for his senior year left the Chieftains' basketball program in shambles.[*]

Emil Sick had signed a working agreement with the Cincinnati Reds. Before long, Fred Hutchinson's front office sent him west to pep up the now-second-division Rainiers. But the celebrating had barely died down in Seattle when Hutch was recalled to the parent club to help reverse the fortunes of the stumbling Reds. After that, stand-in manager Alan Strange could do no better than hand deflated fans a seventh-place finish.

And, horror of horrors, the new *Miss Thriftway* was aced out of yet another Gold Cup by a few ticks of the clock. A five-second difference in elapsed time broke a point-total tie that consigned the hardware to the *Maverick.* Unfortunately, following the 1957 season,

---

[*] Baylor accepted a hefty contract from the Minneapolis Lakers.

owner Bill Waggoner had traded in his Queen City Yacht Club burgee for a flag from Lake Mead. The nomadic cup was destined to be vied for in Nevada in 1960—in a race that was never to be.

Seattle ached.

So was this most spectacular decade in Seattle sports to end on a down note? Far from it. Something was stirring over on the southeastern fringe of the University of Washington campus, and this time the ray of hope *wasn't* emanating from the crewhouse (Coach Ulbrickson had abruptly retired in January). With but a sorry 3-7 record to show for the 1958 season—and with a total of only six wins notched in Jim Owens' belt after two years as head man—the Huskies seemed an improbable source of solace for long-deprived football fans.

Whether the pundits had seen it or not, Owens had accomplished a number of things during the drought. He entered the 1959 campaign with a seasoned nucleus of young men who had graduated with him from the school of hard knocks in '58: Kinnune, Allen, Schloredt, Bullard, Fleming, McKeta, Folkins, Hivner, Claridge, Chapple, Wooten and McKasson. They were conditioned to be tougher than nails and could play the full sixty minutes in a day when the single-platoon system prevailed and substitutions were for pantywaists and certified bleeders. As all comers were soon to learn, they could hit harder than any other team in the country. In the off-season, Owens completed his force with the addition of four key iron men: Ray Jackson, Ben Davidson, John Meyers and Joe Jones. By the end of the first term that brought them all together, they would be known far and wide as the Purple Gang.

The Gang hammered its way to a 9-1 season, the single blemish being a one-touchdown loss to bowl-ineligible Southern California. To many, the invitation to play in Pasadena on New Year's afternoon—one day, admittedly, into the new decade—had the earmarks of a suicide mission. Twelve of the last thirteen Rose Bowl games had gone the way of the Big Ten's representative, and there was no reason to believe the clam diggers from Seattle would do anything to counter this trend against two-touchdown favorite Wisconsin.

Regardless, the Huskies kicked Badger bottoms all over the field from the get-go. In what was arguably the finest, most convincing Rose Bowl win in the school's history—not to mention among the most lopsided on the Tournament of Roses' roll—Washington prevailed 44-8.

The win garnered nationwide respect for Jim Owens' hard-nosed program. It turned Seattle into a football town, a metabolic change that gradually began to steer the spotlight away from other sports it had favored in earlier times. The victory created living legends of the Purple Gang a year before it crafted its master work, a Helms Athletic Foundation national championship.

January 1, 1960, was the topping on a Golden Age in Seattle that gave every sports fan—every citizen—something to cheer about.

# ENCOUNTER WITH A MAVERICK

Bret Maverick was his name, and gambling was his game. He stood tall, six-five or so, and had to duck low to get himself, Stetson and all, out from under the pouring summer rain. He was dressed entirely in black: imposing, alluring, mysterious. But not to a thirteen-year-old kid also escaping the fast-moving shower.

They happened to converge under the protective wing of one of several odd-shaped racing boats gathered in the pits at the foot of Genesee Street, for this was Seattle's biggest event of the year—the Seafair Hydroplane Race on Lake Washington—and Maverick was there to promote a new television series.

It was the summer of 1957: A huge year for hydroplaning and a bigger year for Warner Brothers, the daring filmmaker that was about to unleash *Maverick* to the world that fall.

"Why are you dressed that way?" young Mike asked the tall man standing next to him. He wore a gambler's black jacket over a ruffled white shirt with a black string tie. On his head was a matching black cowboy hat.

"Name's Jim Garner, Sonny" the man responded, bending to fit under the hydro's left wing. "You're looking at my new character on TV, Bret Maverick."

In those days you had to be somebody or know somebody to be in the hydroplane pits. For one, it was a potentially dangerous place, with huge cranes maneuvering the big powerboats into and out of the water, swinging them around to perch on flatbed trucks. For another, the crowds were thick with mechanics, drivers, owners, hangers-on, broadcast and print newsmen and loads of kids, all belonging to someone who needed to be there. In the case of the teen now crouched with Bret under the sponson of a hydroplane, his journalist father took him once a year to see the boats during time trials and collect and trade pins, a primary occupation of visitors to the pits.

So, what connection did this odd, stooped man in black have with hydros? wondered the puzzled boy. He scratched his scalp and scrunched up his face. "Never heard of the TV show yer on. When is it?" he asked the stranger.

"It isn't yet. Comes this fall, on ABC. Sure hope you'll watch it."

Millionaire William T. Waggoner bought the remains of the Rebel, Suh after it hit a floating beer can at a high rate of speed and sank during the 1955 Gold Cup. Rechristened the Maverick and piloted by Bill Stead, the U-12 was just making its mark when the ill-fated hydro exploded and burned on Lake Mead in 1959. Sharing the Maverick brand with ABC's highly rated television series made the boat a crowd-pleaser wherever it competed. (Courtesy of The Hydroplane & Raceboat Museum, Kent, Washington)

To the boy, this was the strangest, weirdest, off-the-cuff advertisement in television history.

"What's it about?"

"Well, I play Bret Maverick ..."

The tall man continued for a few minutes explaining the nature of his character, today considered one of the first and most interesting anti-heroes of that robust black-and-white TV period. Garner was twenty-nine at the time, his birthday being in April, and his show was slated to begin on ABC September 22, which indeed it did. Before it had run its course more than five years later, millions of viewers had watched one hundred twenty-four episodes, in fifty-seven of which Garner appeared, and unintentionally helped ABC erode NBC's position as the second-highest-rated network after CBS.

The squall continued to bulldoze through the Stan Sayers Pits, dedicated just days before on August 5, causing an uncharacteristic heavy downpour for a late July day in Seattle. Another man—one hand over his black head of hair, the other holding a sheaf of papers—bent low to find protection under the boat. He knew the boy, but not his name.

"Hey, young fellow. Hoz'yer dad?"

"Great, Mr. Herring. Hey, this here's Bret Maverick," then turning to the big man, "What was your real name again?"

"James. Jim Garner. I'm an actor."

Chuck Herring was an icon in Seattle at the time, the leading news anchor on the leading news station, KING, which, as an ABC affiliate only until 1958, carried the early episodes of *Maverick*. He was relatively short, personable, approachable, and had a pleasant— one would say, "TV"—demeanor. He shook hands with the cowboy actor and made some unpretentious banter with him, for Herring was not one to be overawed by fame, especially when the fame was *yet to come*.

The storm abated as suddenly as it had materialized. The teen recalled he hadn't gotten a pin from the *Miss Thriftway* or *Wahoo* people yet and saw no reason to tarry.

"Gotta go. See ya, Mr. Herring. See ya … er … Mr. Maverick. Good luck on yer show."

"See ya, kid," was the man in black's response.

The boy scurried away, thinking: *Bret Maverick. Maverick. Funny name for a TV show*, and glanced back at Herring and Garner still chatting under the sponson of the brown-mahogany boat they had used as shelter. Then it struck him. The boat, a favorite on the unlimited hydroplane circuit at the time, *was* the *Maverick*—the U-12 owned by Bill Waggoner, and two years hence as a completely new boat, the U-00, winner of hydroplaning's prestigious Gold Cup.

To the thirteen-year-old, the all-too-brief encounter now made sense.

# DIAL TONES

The idea of reaching out and touching multiple someones on the telephone isn't a novel concept. What *is* new is that contemporary subscribers pay more for the perceived privilege of reaching a wider audience of ears (and now, of course, eyes as well).

In the days when Ma Bell claimed a virtual monopoly on telephone service throughout Seattle and across the nation, the communications colossus offered unlimited local calling minutes and only a slim menu of land-line choices.* One could (A) opt for a "private" line or (B) select what was euphemistically termed a "party" line. The choice determined the customer's basic monthly bill. Mind, in those times, the more ears listening in on one's most intimate conversations, the *less* the cost of the service provided. Conversely, Ma's more bashful subscribers actually paid for the right to exchange secure, two-way chatter on the phone—a notion that today could seem counter-culturish to many.** Really, most people in the Fifties would have been appalled by the thought of yelling their side of a chinfest into an iPhone as they weaved along a crowded downtown sidewalk. That, of course, has all changed.

In the early days of rural telephone exchanges, old-fashioned wall sets frequently accommodated ten-party lines: one crank for the Thoms, two cranks for the Dickeys, two and a half for the Harrimans and so on. By the Fifties, urban service had boiled down to three choices. If a local Bell patron wouldn't ante up for a private line, he or she was looking at a less-expensive two-party hookup, or an even cheaper four-party plan. As regards the last pair of options, heaven

---

* Before cell towers and satellites, millions of miles of telephone wires and cables provided the sole link between the caller and the local deli. Even New Delhi.
** Law enforcement agencies could eavesdrop, but only with rare, legally sanctioned wiretaps.

help all members of the randomly patched network if one or more of the conjoined families counted any number of teenagers vying for the rotary, Western Electric-made kettle phones in use then.

Roger's parents, like many middle-aged Great Depression survivors with kids, pinched the odd penny when it came to overseeing household expenses. The monthly, bare-bones telephone bill (sans today's mysterious universal service taxes and whatnot) was habitually scanned for nonessential long-distance use, which was pretty much limited to notifying family members of the death of someone dear but not necessarily very near. (Telegrams and even cheaper special-delivery letters were popular alternatives to the era's hefty cross-country rates, which shot up even higher during business hours.) Budget-conscious Mom and Dad elected to shave a couple of bucks off their account by selecting two-party service. They did so of their own free wills and the clear understanding that a pair of sons would be the chief users of A.G. Bell's infernal invention. It was all in the name of thriftiness, which, in those times, was almost universally equated with godliness.

Coincidentally, the line the family wound up sharing was with their next-door neighbor, Mrs. Oates, a widow lady seldom seen but for occasions when dogs defecated on her front lawn. (The back was fenced.) Then, she presented herself very publicly as the terror of terriers, the hassler of hounds. Otherwise, she confined herself to her graying 31st Avenue Northeast home doing little, apparently, but sitting by the phone. Hers was the two-short-rings notice to pick up; her neighbor's abode was alerted by a series of long jingles. Being hard of hearing, however (or lonely, as Roger's mother contended), Mrs. Oates was forever answering for both households, to the confusion and consternation of many callers. *Ver*mont/VE 5430 thus became one of the busiest residential lines in north Seattle as eldest son Gary chronically trolled for girlie action using Ma Bell's net. When the line was free, Mrs. Oates gabbed endlessly with another widow named Bessie (or *Messy* Bessie, as the ever-impatient Gary dubbed the stroke-challenged gossip).

Until the late Fifties, local phones required only six twists of the dial to complete a call (and it rightly was dialing then, as opposed to today's button-pushing exercise). VErmont was the telephone prefix that covered the Ravenna district in the northeast corner of town. Mike's family lived just off Latona Avenue near Green Lake and was hooked up to that area's exchange, FIllmore/FI. These were not willy-nilly assignments. The name prefixes defined Seattle's neighborhoods. So much so that if a new coworker offering to join the company bowling team gave a home phone number introduced by GArfield, the captain—without asking—could be pretty sure the enrollee would be driving down from Magnolia. If the prefix was WEst, it was clear to a tenured Seattleite that the kegler had a good idea where the Fauntleroy ferry sailed from.

Roger reached his dad's company on the Western Avenue industrial strip at ELliott 2183. Reserving Greyhound bus tickets for anywhere in the country was as easy as dialing up the depot on Stewart Street at SEneca 3456. Movie times at the Hollywood Theatre in the Roosevelt district could be found at KEnmore 5222 (a prefix shared by the fabled Jolly Roger cabaret and the Coon Chicken Inn farther out on Lake City Way*). Monday morning, a riveter stricken with brown-bottle flu could call in sick at MOhawk 6020, Boeing's Renton plant. Many a wife anxious to track down a wayward husband working on Harbor Island or at Bethlehem Steel was known to phone a popular watering hole on Spokane Street, the Blew Eagle, at HOlly 0211. Old maids at odds with backyard pranksters could reach all three Seattle police precincts at MAin 7810 (911 wouldn't make its appearance until 1971).

But there was one prefix that said everything about Seattle's heart. MUtual plugged into the part of downtown that made it Downtown. To wit, Frederick & Nelson's switchboard was accessed at MU 5500; Ivar Haglund's Acres of Clams, at the foot of Madison (where it is today), could be contacted at MU 2442. For, as every citizen over the age of eight knew then, nothing showcased the town's polished side better than Frango mints and great clam chowder (New England or Manhattan style).

The original Neanderthalic TomTom GPS system, steered by phone numbers themselves, began losing relevance by 1958. Bell saw fit to tack an extra numeral onto the name prefix, thereby stretching line IDs to seven characters. Plain old VErmont might have become, say, VErmont 3 save that the overhaul allowed Ma's people to begin consolidating sequestered neighborhood prefixes into larger, more

---

* Then Bothell Way from East 75th Street out to 145th.

encompassing entities. The revamp also allowed Bell to provide every customer with a private line. With that, VErmont, FIllmore, PLaza (Jules' brand), GLadstone and KEnmore all disappeared under the umbrella of a new, vaster LAkeview—LA with a stick-on number. VE 5430 was now LA 3-5430. MAin guttled ELliott, SEneca, FRanklin, MInor and horned in on some of MUtual's downtown cachet. MElrose got bigger, too and in the southend PArkway and ALpine absorbed LAnder, GIbson, MOhawk, RAinier, LOgan and OLive.

More than the coming of the World's Fair or Seattle's linking to the interstate freeway system in the Sixties, the amalgamation of the prefixes delineating the town's distinctive districts foretold its trending toward big-city status. Never again would a telephone number, by itself, serve as both a compass needle and, often, a rudimentary Dun & Bradstreet rating.

The new name prefixes lasted little more than a decade. The Seventies saw letters give way to all-number tags that, with keen translating skills and a good recall of the old prefixes, might still disclose the general whereabouts of a White Pages listee unwilling to allow his address to be printed in The Book. But by the time mobile phones and BUY-RITE and 800-CRAVING commercial listings came into wide use—when most callers began to punch instead of dial—Mrs. Oates and friend Bessie were communicating with one another from parts unknown.

# ROCKIN' RELIGION AND BROTHER RALPH

Ever since Aimee Semple McPherson built her fire-and-brimstone temples and Elmer Gantry shouted from the silver screen, "Sin, sin, sin! You're all sinners! You're all doomed to perdition!" there's been a cultish love affair with barnstorming evangelical preachers. Every city had them: some enclosed in giant tents ready to come down at the first sign of trouble; others in garish, almost profane palaces that hucksters' money generously paid for.

It was an unusually warm Friday night in April that the lads, always eager to explore Seattle's more mysterious byways, got around to looking up Brother Ralph at his "Million Dollar Church" in Belltown. It was located in the former Consummers [sic] Yeast Company on Battery Street and within sound of the nighttime clatter of Linotype machines inside the huge concrete edifice that was the *Post-Intelligencer* newspaper across Fifth Avenue to the north.

Now, it's fair to say Mike and Roger had long heard about the Seattle Revival Center, because its "entertainment value" had been bandied about among peripheral friends all winter long, and more out of curiosity than skepticism they decided to scope it out.

Roger parked the family's Ford under the newly constructed Monorail along Fifth and, with Mike in tow, let his lanky legs set a determined stride southeast along Battery. It wasn't difficult to find the entry way to the holy temple because, from several yards out, one could hear a rockin' refrain coming from within.

*Are you washed in the blood,*
*In the soul-cleansing blood of the Lamb?*
*Are your garments spotless? Are they white as snow?*
*Are you washed in the blood of the Lamb?*

Just inside the outer door they entered a glittering foyer of lights and literature. A black man, with a face craggy from years of boxcar travel and too many roll-yer-owns, but dressed neatly in a slightly tattered suit coat and skinny black necktie, greeted the boys with a gnarled hand and a folded handout for each.

"Welcome. Please join us. There's plenty of room. So glad you could come along," he said in a gravelly voice.

Roger and Mike didn't know quite what to think of the invitation. Somewhat intimidated, they weren't sure they really wanted to commit to going inside and becoming an accomplice to the festivities; instead, they considered hanging loose at the entrance to observe, not so much out of respect but out of fear of the unknown. But before they knew it, they were ushered into a room where a sparse audience sat scattered among three sets of church pews separated by two aisles of threadbare reddish carpet.

Those attending were mostly old and gray, and for the most part African-American, and they all faced an altar of radiant candles and strings of colored electric lights where at that moment a youngish white man with slicked-back black hair and Brooks Brothers suit was raising a leather-bound book he clutched in his right hand, his head deeply bowed, his eyes tightly closed.

"Are *you* washed in the blood of the lamb?" he was emphasizing. "Join me. Rejoice with me. Don't join this generation of vipers, Satan's sworn fornicators and whoremongers. Don't let the great serpent win. Rejoice in the Lord, and you, too, will be glad. Let us pray...."

And just like that there was a righteous rush of sound in that opulent space as the worshipers bent forward or slipped down between the pews to pray, their knees touching the parquet floor.

The boys, having found four seats halfway up one of the aisles, bowed their heads, too—not to pray, for they still didn't know what to make of the scene, but so as not to look conspicuous.

Following the prayer came another tune—not your off-key "What a friend we have in Jesus" melody, but a rock-'em-sock-'em gospel song more akin to Mount Zion Baptist Church up in the predominately black Central District. The music was directed on stage by a young white couple, he in a powder-blue suit, ruffled shirt and string tie and she in a yellowish blouse and full, peach-colored, circle-cut skirt. Keeping time was a small organ, a two-manual Kimball.

Roger and Mike, standing with everyone else, clapped hesitatingly along with the music but didn't sing. For one, they had never heard such a tune before, and two, keeping track of what was going on stretched their concentration levels to the max.

Suddenly, about halfway through the third verse, an ancient woman with a feathery cloche hat cried out, "Hee-yah! Hee-yah!" All eyes became riveted on her. "Hee-yah! Hee-yah!" she shouted again, pointing to the front of the tiny church. "I sees Jesus! I sees Jesus, there in the corner. Hee-yah!"

The boys almost lost it. But the adrenaline coursed through them, keeping them from bursting into noticeable guffaws that without doubt would've caused the tar and feathers to come out.

After the apparition was duly noted, the woman began doing a fast-step dance up the short aisle. Two or three others joined her. A moment later, a frenzy of jumpin' and jivin' with Jesus was going on within and without the area around the pews. The organ doubled its volume. This went on for several minutes and culminated with the small group of men and women congregated in the aisles, dancing around as though in a juke joint rather than the House of the Lord.

When the celebrants quieted down, Ralph took on a somber state, gripped tight his black book and without a word began to pray. After a moment of pure silence, he grinned at his audience and proclaimed: "I rejoice in the Lord, and I am glad."

"Hallelujah!" shouted the black woman from her place. "Hee-yah!"

For days and weeks, the boys could talk of little else but that eye-opening experience at the Seattle Revival Center. They told their friends about it to the point that several of them wanted to see the "show" for themselves.

So, the first Friday in May, Roger and Mike gathered a few pals for a drive to Belltown. Along were Jules, always up for a lark but this time claiming he was only keen on "hearing the vibes, man"; a gung-ho, but reticent, acquaintance named Jim; and Hugh, who insisted on escorting them all in his Rambler American. By Roosevelt High's priggish standards, Hugh was regarded as something of an eccentric and class cut-up. If inspired, there seemed to be no limit to what he would do to get a laugh, and he never shunned the opportunity to be a key player in some stunt or other. Early on, the lads learned one didn't dare dare Hugh—or *Huey* when he was on a roll—to do anything a certifiably insane person would be inclined to do.

Recognized as having been there before, Mike and Roger received a welcome with special ardor that night. The craggy host at the door opened a smile so wide one could easily count the five teeth he had; one of the deacons grabbed a hand in both of his and squeezed so hard Roger thought he'd have to turn physical to get away; a sub-preacher, called to the entryway, pulled the two aside to briefly interrogate their purpose and learn more about who the others were; he was quickly appeased, grateful for the growing congregation. After all, this was a special night at the "Million Dollar Church," for a young woman was to be baptized during the proceedings.

The audience was particularly full and frenetic this night. The day had been near sixty as spring made its first full showing of the year, and people were out and about, enjoying the clean air and evening breeze. Many of them migrated to the Seattle Revival Center, either through habit or just because it was there. And the Lord was with them and ready to boogie.

The five boys took their places in a middle pew on the right side. Shortly after the first song, a stirring rendition of "Rock of Ages," Hugh had a brainstorm. A registered Catholic who had transferred to Roosevelt from Seattle Prep for his senior year (to the utter relief of both him and the good fathers), the newcomer decided he was in need of a second baptizing. Not only that, but a look to the left convinced him that Roger should be born again along with him. The whispered suggestion filled Roger with fear and loathing, but always a sucker for a challenge, he gritted teeth and agreed to it. Huey raised both of their hands to seal the deal, nudged Roger into the aisle and hustled both of them toward the proscenium shouting, "We want to believe!" They were quickly ushered to the right of the sanctuary where they disappeared from view, taking a hidden staircase that led to the church's attic.

Roger suddenly felt the sheer terror of what Huey so spontaneously had gotten him into, for he had an inkling this would be no light tap of holy water on the forehead and a few Hail Marys!, or whatever they said. This would be the real deal, and like a clairvoyant in a spooky sideshow, he strangely saw himself lying nose down, perhaps drowned, in a baptism pool.

For that's exactly what it would be: a full-immersion baptism in four feet of water kept under a set of floorboards in front of the altar. Roger's first clue into what the ritual entailed struck him when he arrived in the "changing room" high in the rafters. There, above the din of more muffled hymns, he and Huey were given white sailor suits two sizes too small and told to strip to their underwear and put them on. "What the hell?" he uttered. Soon they joined the young woman—about seventeen, who all sober and sweet had emerged from behind a partition dressed in a white muslin robe. The three, led by one of the ushers, made the slow journey down the creaky stairs to the right of the stage where they were lined up in full view of the worshipers a step behind a tub of rank-looking liquid.

First there were solemn prayers, with Brother Ralph presiding, his black holy tome raised high in the air. Then a few riffs from the organ. The woman in peach even came up to the stage microphone and in a delicate soprano voice sang a quick ditty invoking Jesus as their one true savior, to which was often heard "hallelujahs," "praise Gods" or "hee-yas!" from the congregation.

Then came the dunking—not by Brother Ralph but two attendants in waders. First the young woman stepped into the fetid water and was thrown unceremoniously backward, almost topsy-turvy, into the water. After a harrowing moment, she came up with the first two fingers of her left hand tightly pinching her nose. Then it was time for Huey, whom they quickly flopped down. He wasn't under for long but came up violently, gasping for air and uttering what seemed to be the word "Geronimo!" but too difficult to make out under the crowd's loud, ecstatic zeal.

Roger was next and Mike was sorely afraid. This would be Roger's undoing, he speculated. He noticed Huey already was smiling, luridly. Could his friend hold his composure? Indeed, could he even hold his water?

Suddenly, Ralph began to do his thing again, perhaps with more vigor than before, like performing an exorcism. The attendant stepped up and pulled Roger backward into the well-used bath water and seemed to hold him there for a longer time than was necessary. When let go, Roger rose from the pool in a manner resembling a whale's breach, spraying the foul fluid all over the stage, the attendants, Miss Fluffy Skirt and Brother Ralph and his Brooks Brothers suit.

Mike, Jules and Jim could hardly contain themselves, and as the audience began jiving to the crescendoing organ, each buried his face in his arms across the back of the pew, as though openly weeping, and laughed until tears actually did fill their eyes.

And just like that the service was over. Roger, Huey and the Young Believer sloshed up the backstage staircase to towel off and dress in their civvies. The others quickly made their way out onto the street to wait, smoke and distance themselves from the departing worshipers.

They had done it. They had made it through the ordeal without faltering. They had kept their cool and not undone what certainly would've spelled a rail parade up Battery Street.

Soon, Roger and Huey emerged. Both seemed more somber than usual. Neither said a word, even after reaching the sidewalk.

Once in the car, though, the laughter began, first from Mike who could not hold back and then from Jim who kept slapping Huey on the shoulder, yelling, "You did it! You did it! I can't believe it! You guys are kerrrazy!" Jules in the back seat was popping tops off Oly stubbies and chuckling in his own softer way, but obviously in great admiration of the stunt.

Huey, the stress level subsided, broke into a prolonged guffaw, accepted a proffered beer and slid down behind the Rambler's steering wheel. "Best damn bath I ever had. Yeah, real cool!"

Hugh started the car and set off down Fifth listening to Jules' directions to West Seattle. Only Roger, who sat in front slowly chewing his first sips of beer, was abnormally quiet.

# THE JUMP

Members of the RHS Class of 1962 were flirting with dotage when Pulitzer Prize-winner David Horsey wrote, pointedly:

> I am very familiar with Roosevelt. For many decades, it has remained one of the city's top high schools, in large part because of the active support of the affluent community that has, for generations, claimed the school as its own.
>
> There is only one negative side to this sense of ownership. The school's social scene has long been dominated by a clique that likes to set the rules and choose the insiders and outsiders. These social arbiters tend to be the overindulged kids who expect to get a new sports car for their 16th birthdays and who are destined to spend their college years binge drinking on Greek Row.[*]

Without realizing it, Horsey's thesis at least partially explains why The Jump never became an indispensable piece of Roosevelt High legend.

Had Kurt Cobain lived back when, odds are he would never have drawn inspiration for his generation's cachet, "Smells Like Teen Spirit," from the Where-Were-You-in-Sixty-two crowd out on Fifteenth and Sixty-sixth. To the cream puffs in charge of zeitgeist that year, letting it all hang out meant ordering onions on after-the-game cheeseburgers. Even the venerable school nickname, Roughriders, was eroding away to the namby-pamby sobriquet The Teddies. (And a *teddy*, as Jules was fond of reminding his comrades, was a piece of intimate feminine apparel—underwear, with a snap

[*] From David Horsey's *Burning Question* column appearing in the *Seattle Post-Intelligencer*, November 26, 2005, used with his permission.

crotch. Viewed in that sense, the trendy new pet name said loads about the wussification of its student body.)

Yet earlier, Sand Point scions had countenanced, even quietly plotted, class pranks. A couple of years before, the seniors had successfully conspired to check out every book in the school's library. Not to be outdone, the Class of Sixty-one contrived to secretly cache nearly a thousand wind-up alarm clocks in hundreds of lockers around the building—all set to chime at 2:30 P.M. It wasn't the stuff of Cal Poly trickery, to be sure. But these polite capers did manage to plant fertile seeds sprouting at least a hint of that intangible tangible called school spirit, along with memories that would draw bigger guffaws at each succeeding reunion.

However, the year of the World's Fair found inspiration of any kind at a low ebb. Small wonder when looking back at a preppy senior class whose lasting legacy would be the avoidance of getting its teddy in a bunch.

Enter The Jumper and what might have been.

That afternoon, a sickly breeze barely ruffled the leaves on the fabled gingko trees out front. The unusually hot and heavy May air was layered in such a way that every odor along a two-block stretch of Fifteenth Northeast pooled into one great, invisible stink that stuck on the face of the adjacent building twenty feet above the pavement. One of the sweating inmates confined to Room 233 on the east side attempted to spare his fellow prisoners death from heat stroke by raising the window nearest the vacant teacher's desk. He bowed and took his seat to cautious applause, unaware that the open sash, like a huge ladle, was drawing in the polluted soup outside.

A Truman-era Hudson with Blackie Carbon-ized rings laid a thick vapor trail down the street below. The tailpipe's discharge of cremated Bardahl topoil and fifty-weight Oilzum mingled, then mated, with the afternoon's last gasp from the grease-coated griddles in Maryanne's and, across the street, at the Roughrider. The piquancy north of Sixty-fifth was crowned with the not-so-subtle essence of cigarette smoke belching from the open door of alternative dining's Dusty's, where the dented Rock-Ola jukebox never shut up. All of it found a home inside the imposing brick oven already under assault by olfactory offenders emanating from the lunchroom downstairs.

Mike subconsciously thumb-bongoed something Sandy Nelsonish on a hoary desktop hand-engraved with profundities like

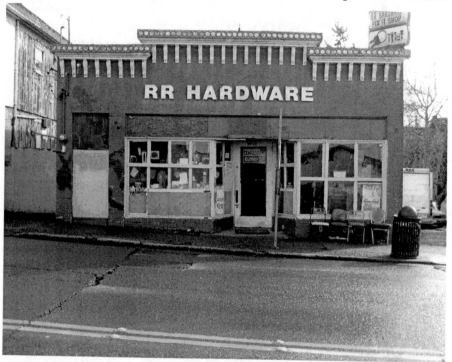

Decades ago there were a number of nearby options open to Roosevelt Teddies weary of school lunchroom victuals—or in need of a smoke break. The wayward Dusty's on 15th Avenue Northeast and 66th occupied half of the building pictured. While definitely unsuited to the Dick and Deedee set, the smoking lamp was always alight for the ciggie and Coke crowd during school hours. (R. Miller photo)

"Lynx are loosers" [sic] and "Beavers gopher Beavers." He sighed the sigh of a lost soul incarcerated in the world's deepest dungeon. The usually redlining internal dynamo that powered him barely showed a charge in the mind-smothering heat. He had already unbuttoned his chartreuse short-sleeve to the waist, only to run out of breath blowing hot air down the inside of his T-shirt. Nothing helped. The temperature didn't fall and the day's crushing inertia wouldn't lift.

Mike was losing his mind, just like the fat guy they had read about in W.F. Harvey's "August Heat." Except a couple of months early.

He carefully rubbed away the moisture collecting in the corners of his tearing eyes. A pioneering contacts wearer, Mike's hard lenses today seemed bent on attracting and sealing in every bit of microscopic crud swirling around north Seattle. He repeatedly blinked at the notice boldly chalked on the blackboard and, with nothing else to do, began putting the message to a Brubeck beat.

## CLASS
**Mr. Grey has been taken ill. A substitute teacher is being dispatched and will join you presently. In the meantime, remain seated and continue with the day's lesson in your reader.**
## DO NOT OPEN THE WINDOWS

Yeah, yeah.

Mike's fidgeting right foot unintentionally tapped his pulverized copy of *Gems of British Poetry* into the aisle between desks. His eyes left the blackboard while he retrieved the book, then caught the lifeless wall clock on the way back up. Its hands were glued to 1:24. As he slumped in his seat, Mike drew in a lungful of the dead air and let it ferment down deep.

It wasn't clear why Mr. Grey now seemed content with exhibiting the traffic-stopping charisma of Wally Cox. In another life he had been a battle-ready citizen soldier who was still paying dues for his part in fighting the Japanese in World War II. Like so many other veterans of the South Pacific theater, an evil mosquito had seen to it that he returned to the States with a lasting memento of the grueling campaign. Mr. Grey's recurring bouts with malaria were not uncommon: also unpredictable, unpreventable and ordinarily debilitating within an hour or two of the onset. The grapevine feed from fourth period had pretty well telegraphed news of the latest episode to incoming classes. Nothing, however, could have prepared Mike for today's head-on collision with eighteen-wheeled tedium.

The time machine was stuck in compound low, going nowhere: deadsville, but for the sound of flies buzzing and sweat dripping. It felt to Mike like what a Catholic buddy described as purgatory, or listening to Shorty Templeman lose yet another Indy 500 over the Mutual Network. Geez Loueeez, a guy should be out there— *anywhere* out there—tackling pressing problems that involved earning a buck; washing his car; solving real puzzles like finding a cure for hiccups.

For a moment, Mike fancied he could hear Chuck Berry's "School Days" wafting up from Dusty's:

*Workin' your fingers right down to the bone,*
*And the guy behind you won't leave you alone....*

At the time, nary a soul attending Roosevelt felt concerned about being physically molested, unless turning out for the sorry football program headed by Lou Hull. Socioeconomic boundaries were so clearly defined at the school that duking it out to become king (or queen) of the hill was seen as an outmoded bad habit soon shed by survivors of Eckstein and Marshall Junior Highs, if they expected to make the grade at RHS. Even Big Ed, imposing All-Everything lineman on the ninth-place team in the expanding league, was a pussycat off the gridiron. He was snoring softly now, as he so often did after lunch, and drooling just enough to cool off his hairy right wrist. The only thing for classmates to fear from Ed was getting in his way following the stroke of the dismissal bell. Mike, seated but a dozen feet from the door, had been run over more than once in the daily dash for the exit. Even Roosevelt's greatest ball-handling basketball guard was no match for the freedom-bound, one-man stampede.

But today, things would be different.

Other captives in the Grey Room combated boredom by milling about the civilized cage. Everybody who was anybody (and craved the company of clones) gravitated toward the back where they couldn't be readily seen by prying eyes peering through the glass inserts in the door. The boys who looked like members of the Kingston Trio and the girls doubling for Sandra Dee—spawn of Laurelhurst's Tanqueray and tonic set—hung near the back wall to pitch deodorized woo and decide whether to drive Mom's Caddy or Daddy's Mark II to the prom.

The chosen few represented the leadership of a list of prestigious school organizations that, in abbreviated form, could have passed for the departmental directory of the British Home Office: the ASR, RHO, BC, MYP, JOG, IHC, MAP, GIC, the Q and S, and, honest-to-Gidget, still another called Spruffs. The well-coiffed folk who served as COs were, naturally, Roosevelt's movers and shakers. (Mike and his closest friends were affiliated only with AU—Alcoholics Unanimous.) Mr. Grey's class was packed with the smart set hailing from the right (east) side of Thirty-fifth Northeast. (Mike was a proud veteran of John Marshall, which drew heavily from the blue-collar Latona neighborhood.) The swells with a view of Lake Washington expected snappy curbside service at the Burg. (Mike would have crawled a mile to Dag's or Dick's following Friday-night frolics in West Seattle.) The entitled from birth were into the Fleetwoods and The Brothers Four. (Mike was a Ray Charles kind of cat who could belt out "What'd I Say" better than any other white kid in Seattle—when Rockin' Robin Roberts wasn't in town.)

Like most of the unanointed, Mike had spent the bulk of his high school sentence flying under Sand Point's radar. But beginning early in his senior year, a series of unpremeditated PR triumphs began jeopardizing the handy low profile that allowed him easy access to a wide variety of activities in and outside of school. He had starred for a second time in the Roosevelt Revue, won best supporting actor in the ballyhooed Drama Festival, and his rock 'n' roll combo had been hired to play not one but two dances arranged by swinging (within reason) senior-class sophisticates. All year, he had been spotted taking turns walking two dishy girls in the halls (one of them said to be jailbait), and very recently had been ID'd behind the wheel of a very cool white 1955 Studebaker Commander equipped with seat belts. Secondhand reports from slumming patricians alleged that he could sometimes be seen late at night playing the Hammond organ at a beatnik enclave in the U-District called the Café Encore; that he seemed to be able to perform from memory Top Fifty curiosities like "Take Five" and "Like Young."

Without scoring a touchdown, serving as class president or batting three-hundred, Mike was being noticed by fellows named Cappy, Chap, Cope and Con. But, really, what was he—actor, rocker, bohemian (though some had even heard Eagle Scout), legitimate musician, good-time Charlie: *what*? Yet the likes of Chip the Third never bothered to ask him, and Mike went his merry way being an enigma to all of them.

He pulled hard on both earlobes in the hope it would keep his eyes open as he fought off a willful yawn. From under burning lids he sized up the clutch of cheerleaders, embedded jocks, recording secretaries, cotillion queens and junior country clubbers. It was difficult to fathom how one middling English class had managed to accumulate such a concentration of them. Another yawn pried at Mike's jaws and this time he let it have its way. The zitless people were in their element over by the windows: urbane at eighteen, blithely schmoozing, not a dirty fingernail or hint of bad breath among them.

The pixie girl with a headache band running through her blonde hair just above the bangs—the best skier of the bunch—glanced Mike's way with a look that could have withered the Amazon jungle. All of it, in under a minute. Her expression inspired Mike to quietly hum a few bars of Laurie London's old hit accompanied by soundless, modified lyrics that ran, "She's got the whole wide world by the balls." A third yawn repressed the need to finish the primitive protest song, and the skier turned her attention to showing off a new pair of imported pumps to the peerage.

Time crawled on in slow motion. The clock's sickly hands had made it as far as 1:28 and simply died there. Two seats back, Big Ed was making noises that mimicked the death rattle of a rock crusher. Mike cleared a sticky throat in sympathy with his crew-cut competition for low-grade honors in Mr. Grey's class. The thought of finals lurking just around the corner began to rouse him from his stupor. Jules was bugging him daily to get started on his application to attend the University of Washington in the fall. But being behind in virtually every class this semester by at least a report and three chapters of something, Mike wasn't entirely sure that 1962 would mark the last year he darkened the fusty halls of Roosevelt High. If not, he wondered whether he would be allowed to appear in the Sixty-three Revue as a senior Senior; for that matter, attend the prom again when he and his latest squeeze would be in the same graduating class. And, cripers, that reminded him of the ten-dollar deposit he had yet to drop off at Brocklind's reserving the powder blue (or was it pewter blue?) tux jacket his junior sweetie had inveigled him into wearing to the Big Hoedown at the HUB in June. Dolly had come to view their casual dating as a steady relationship now—exclusive, too, as in demanding no more class-cutting to wander around Cowen Park with worldly-wise Tess. That wasn't all. Dolly was making more and more demands on what little spare time Mike had all the while boss Warren Ghormley was leaning on him to increase his weekend hours at Dick's. The latest from his ball-and-chain was pressure to take her to a sappy *Lover Come Back-Light in the Piazza* double feature after what promised to be a grueling all-day band practice in the dungeon at KOMO Radio tomorrow. After shaking down his drummer for union dues and fighting with the guitar player over adding "You Can't Sit Down" to the group's repertoire, Mike knew damn well that his heart would be crying out for Olys with the lads and a backrow seat to see *Walk on the Wild Side* at the Kenmore Drive-In.

1:32. In four minutes, Mike had gone from merely simmering in brick-oven heat to stewing in his own juice. He clawed at his mushy underarms and collected a Mona Lisa smile from the nearsighted girl to his left who read Tolstoy for pleasure. She was in his next-hour German class, too, and ... and then the full horror of the insufferable afternoon came around to look him square in his red eyes. Riding out the next thirty-plus minutes, if it could be done—"...remain seated and continue the day's lesson..."—promised no respite, for there was still the awful, interminable expanse of sixth period yet to be endured. What would be dished up in there today that would make Lizzie Borden crazy all over again?—the corny, "Hey, kids, I have a pebble in my shoe" routine, or "Ich bin unter dem Tische," as the goofball often greeted them from under a table near the door while they entered the cabinet of Herr Professor Dummkopf.

Now a terminal nic fit was rearing its ugly head and hissing at him. Mike hadn't inhaled a Viceroy (with "The Thinking Man's Filter") since noon when he had left the pack lying on his car's front seat way down Sixty-eighth off the east coast of Hawaii. His left eyelid was twitching uncontrollably when the owner of a passing Buick convertible tapped out "Colonel Bogey" on its horn. The Teddees and Teddettes by the windows warmed their palms in tepid appreciation and ...

Snap. Just a very little *snap*.

As Steve McQueen's character, Vin, explains in *The Magnificent Seven*, "It seemed to be the right idea at the time." In a millisecond, Mike knew what *It* was and why *It* had to be done.

The chattering across the room leveled off, then fell down a deep hole. Mike stood up and made for the open window. The nearsighted girl put down *Anna Karenina* and stared at the blurry outline of her classmate as he slipped off his right shoe, then his left. A shoulder jab delivered by the basketball star brought Big Ed back to life in time to see Mike thoughtfully placing his battered loafers on the sill.

"Gees, Eddy, I think the piano player's gonna jump," the hoopster croaked as Mike was leaning far out the open window to study the grounds two stories below.

Big Ed arranged himself so that he could pass gas without being heard. "No, he's gonna make it *look* like he jumped," he judged correctly. "Oh, Momma!"

Mike spared no one so much as a glance in spite of the rising buzz and a vivid awareness that every eye in the room was on him. With all the confidence of a best supporting actor, he turned and padded for the door in his stocking feet.

"Shit-o-dear, he's flipped out," the lone student from auto shop dared say.

"No." The nearsighted girl who had been sneaking looks at Mike all semester shook her head emphatically. "No, he knows exactly what he's doing," she told thirty-two sets of ears that weren't listening.

The civilized klatsch, clustered in the far corner, was restive but mum. The seditious act of walking out of class and heading off downstairs was just too far outside the fixed orbit of accepted DeMolay and Scrapbook Committee conduct to be condoned. By crossing the line and going AWOL, Mike had sentenced himself to excommunication by the Windermere chapter of the Vatican. Well, as the song went, "Que Sera, Sera."

During his extracurricular outings with Tess, he had discovered that the building always seemed to be swaddled in a security-lax torpor come most early afternoons. Today was no different, and Mike descended to the north entrance alone and unchallenged. Once outside, he squinted up at the face of the building to get his bearings, exercising care not to step too far away from the building to be noticed by students in the ground-floor rooms. Tipping his hand to anyone would spell a hasty end to his greatest inspiration since getting himself permanently excused from gym. He hopped off the stoop and slunk to a spot directly below the second-story window from which even the most bird-brained substitute could only conclude he had fallen—or jumped. Mike arranged himself, facedown, like a Rorschach blot on the narrow pathway and waited.

Roosevelt had nearly succeeded, slowly but surely, in boring him to death over what was coming up on three years of confinement. As with many other nimble minds before and after him, the high school experience at Teddy Town had served only to sedate and stultify almost every creative urge born within its walls. It was so infernally easy to glide through one's so-called academic career in the button-down world of Roosevelt—no pantsings, no lunchroom food fights, no cherry bombs in the toilets—being fed a steady diet of civility served up with gobs of tractable Pabulum. Small wonder Mike's most productive hours had been spent far away from flatulent scholasticism, cruising Alki and the darkened back streets of West Seattle to find voice for his thoughts, absorbing culture at the Latvian House and the Encore, cultivating tastes at the Varsity Theatre and hatching ideas in KOMO's Studio G, inventing himself in school-sanctioned projects *only* if they happened after 3:10 P.M. But it had been a close call, for Roosevelt's stealthy brand of lobotomy had narrowly missed bushwhacking Mike several times over the long haul—until today. Today was payback time.

Revolutionary zeal aside, his head began to hurt the longer he lay there. Actually, it was his nose and right cheek that pained him where the rough cement had begun making little craters in still-tender teen skin. No matter. Jerking himself straight and flipping over, he aimed a broad smile at the cheerful blue sky until his gaze was arrested by Big Ed's big face jutting out of the open window twenty feet above him. Big Ed looked worried even at that distance and his palpable concern immediately transferred itself to the dead body come back to life on the ground below.

"Lookout says somebody's coming," the block of granite had just enough time to call down to Mike. "Lookout says ..."

"TAKE YOUR SEAT!" a voice braced with far more testosterone than Ed's boomed behind him.

Ed jumped, smacking the back of his close-cropped head on the bottom of the window frame before pulling his torso inside. "But listen," Mike heard him try to explain. "You gotta look down there, Sir—*Ma'am*. There's been an accident and ..."

Without a glance outside, the study hall warden most called the Old Battle-ax slammed the window shut with the force of an atomic pile driver. She had been deprived of a second cup of coffee and a third cigarette during her routine fifth-period sabbatical in the teacher's lounge, and the class she had been drafted to subdue was going to pay dearly for her sacrifice. "ALL OF YOU—TAKE YOUR SEATS! *NOW!*"

Mike plainly heard her, right through the outer wall of the building, laying down the law to her cowering charges. He reacted as one with his classmates, though deviating from the drill by jumping to attention rather than diving for cover. An as-yet-unacculturated sophomore boy in Room 123 gave him the finger when his head popped into view. Mike failed to notice the rude gesture because his rumpled brain had jammed trying to devise a way to back out of a caper that had totally gone off the tracks.

He faced the entrance with the kind of enthusiasm reserved for midterms. By the time he got around to opening it, the specter of suspension, or worse, had sucked all the wind right out of him. Mike reached the last of the steps in the second flight of stairs like a condemned man who was arriving early for his appointment with the gallows. Turning the corner, it was at once obvious that the jig was up, for the door to Mr. Grey's classroom stood wide open as if expressly inviting his return.

At the sight of the shoeless student, the substitute crossed in front of the teacher's desk with unshaven legs thrashing inside a long skirt better suited to gunnysack racing. Her hands were hidden away in back of her and, when she stopped to give Mike a visual dressing-down, there was a lot of Margaret Hamilton and a pinch of Robert Newton playing Long John Silver in her practiced glower. The Old Battle-ax had verbally savaged everyone in the room by now, yet there was still plenty of venom left to spare for this tall, skinny miscreant.

Mike took in all the air he could hold and did his best to steady himself for the grilling.

"And where," came the inevitable opener, "have *you* been?"

He was ready for that: "I had to go to the can—the restroom."

The no-nonsense sub cut him no slack and whipped out her concealed hands to present each of the gnarly loafers. "And what are *these*?"

Mike was ready for that, too: "I'd say they're shoes. *My* shoes."

Her sly right eye narrowed to a slit. "And why were they left on the window sill during your absence?"

Mike had not quite finished readying himself for that particular line of questioning. "Well ... because ..." was as far as he got.

"*Because*?" The acting commandant puffed up as she prepared to lower the boom.

They had never been close friends. But the auto shop whiz at the back of the class had known Mike since the second grade at Green Lake Elementary. They had played a lot of marbles one summer, though, and the cat's-eyes he had won from Mike still filled an empty jam jar next to his tool box in the family garage. "*Because*," the budding mechanic lied fearlessly, "Mister Grey makes the boys leave their shoes in the room when they gotta go. That way, they have to come back and get 'em. He was just following the rules."

Big Ed swallowed a laugh while the O.B. savored Mr. Grey's commendable—if absolutely fictitious—administering of discipline. In a weak moment, she opted not to chastise the buttinsky's outspokenness and let Mike off with an uncharacteristic, if curt, "Button your shirt and take your seat."

Mike's shoes were dropped on the floor like plague-carrying rats before she turned away. He slipped them on but didn't complete the order until reaching the security of his desk. As he was aligning the first hole with the bottom button, the myopic girl leaned over to whisper, "Darned nice try."

Word of The Jump—most of it incoherent or wildly embellished to the point of misidentifying the perp—had reached all corners of the school by early the next week. Mr. Grey didn't even connect the incident with his classroom when he overheard a garbled rehashing in the teachers' sanctum at Monday lunch. Rumors were so widespread by Tuesday that the eastern gentry felt compelled to put its own spin on the escapade to quash any ideas that antisocial deeds, other than those insiders fantasized about, had occurred on its watch. The story was "leaked" to the in-crowd's mouthpiece, the weekly *Roosevelt News*, where a cooperative editor cowrote a sanitized piece titled, "Is It True???". The exposé alleged:

> Last week when a certain teacher was absent his fifth period class decided to pull a joke on the substitute.
>
> When the substitute left the room for a few minutes, the boy took off his shoes, placed them on the window sill and then ran down to the ground floor and pretended he had fallen out of the window.
>
> When the teacher returned, the class was standing by the window and they were told to sit down.
>
> The good-natured substitute just laughed the joke off and soon the brave boy who jumped from the second floor window returned to finish his studying.

Leonard, Jules, Johns and Roger refused, on principle, to read the *Gnus* [sic] and relied on Mike's fluffless account told over copious beers in the wilds north of Richmond Beach. Big Ed and the nearsighted girl each asked Mike to sign their *Strenuous Life* annuals. Mike's grade-school playmate unexpectedly landed an apprentice mechanic's job at a Plymouth-Dodge dealership on Aurora and cut his last week and a half of classes to work. The Jump got to be old news, then no news at all, when a stolen twenty-pound fire extinguisher disgorged itself inside a coed's locker on the first floor.

Soon after that, with little fanfare, the Roosevelt dog-and-pony show ended for all of them. There were no refunds.

# TASTING THE DIFFERENCE AT DICK'S

Mike couldn't drive until he was eighteen, owing more to the fact that neither of his parents drove than because he was a menace on the road. He had his Schwinn, the Green Phantom, that got him places when he needed to be there.

When he turned sixteen, he decided to change careers. Up till then, his entrepreneurial spirit had led him to sell handmade Christmas table decorations and name-embossed cards, as well as household items created by blind people he had never seen, and there was hardly a neighborhood in Seattle he and his Schwinn didn't know intimately. But it was time, now that he was of legal age, to get a real job.

Hearing about potential work eleven blocks south of his home, he mounted the Phantom and pedaled down Latona to Forty-fifth Street and over to a six-year-old fast-food restaurant that was growing in reputation, particularly among high school and college kids. There was nothing like it around.

Ray Kroc arguably became the best-known king of cheap hamburgers when he turned a small-town drive-in restaurant into an international superchain known as McDonald's. But while Kroc was the monarch of Mickey D's, Dick Spady and Warren Ghormley stand out as commanders-in-chief of the real "Big D"—Dick's Drive-in—a bastion for burger lovers that opened in Seattle, Washington, four hundred forty-two days before the first official McDonald's.

The date was January 28, 1954, and the place was Wallingford—111 East 45th Street, to be precise—but a second Dick's opened one year later at 115 Broadway North on Capitol Hill. Both stores, with relatively few cosmetic changes from the early days, do goldmine business even today, as do the other four locations along Holman Road, at Lake City, on lower Queen Anne and most recently on Old

99 near the city of Edmonds. The motto, then and now, is: "Dick's, where TASTE is the difference."

What sparked its popularity more than anything else were its prices and simplicity. Until 1971, all you could get were burgers and cheeseburgers; hand-dipped vanilla, strawberry and chocolate milkshakes; French fries; and soft drinks, coffee and milk—oh, and hot-fudge sundaes sold at a separate window. The burgers for the first several years were nineteen cents, five cents more for the cheese, and they all came with a splat of mustard and ketchup, no exceptions. Later, Spady and Ghormley (and a third-but-silent partner, Prof. Tom Thomas) would add a "special" burger and "deluxe" cheeseburger to the menu.

A badge of honor and pride can be worn by the multitude of young people who over the years have worked for Dick's as a first job. Today, the company offers kids scholarships, as well as healthcare benefits and even 401Ks. It is, and always has been, a great place to work.

And so would Mike find out.

Parking the Schwinn out back, he knocked gently on the heavy door and was ushered into an untidy back room, strung with white cooks' uniforms and bins for street clothes, and down a narrow hallway to Ghormley's neat-as-a-pin office. The co-owner, tall and gaunt with remarkably thick graying hair, welcomed the young guest and had him sit next to the desk. Questions and answers, from both sides, led to an understanding, and Mike was in, starting Friday night, as a fry cook.

If you were a young man, you always began as a fry cook. The preparation never varied: dump spuds from chute into tumbler lined with abrasive stripping for ten minutes or so; take potato in left hand and set it in a mechanical dicing machine; pull down handle allowing raw potato strips to fall into soaking-sink and repeat many times, avoiding as best you can dicing your fingers by not removing them quickly enough. After the potatoes soaked all day, they would be transferred to another sink and eventually to the fry basket, which was dropped as sales warranted into hot vegetable oil. Once the fries were cooked, they could be deposited under a heat lamp and well salted. A bottomless scoop allowed the cook to pick up just enough crispy fries to fill a hand-held envelope bag. These went for eleven cents each and were among the most popular purchases at any Dick's. The whole process on the right side of the store was carefully overseen by "Top Steer," a huge white-faced bull shown in a painting hanging on the back wall.

Burgers were easier. One pulled down a tray of pre-prepared and measured patties and flopped them on a flat grill, depending on how many were needed at the moment in quantities of twelve, twenty-four or thirty-six. Buns were laid on the griddle as well, and when toasted, they were spread out in neat rows on the stainless-steel counter and dolloped with mustard and ketchup from hand-held, trigger-activated dispensing cones. The quality of the cook was measured not by how many burgers he (in those days, only boys did this job) could prepare but in how fast he could wrap them. It took little practice to learn how to fold and fling the maximum number of wrapped burgers in less than one minute.

The ice-cream section was the home of the Dick's female employees in the early Sixties. They are responsible for dipping the ice cream into metal shake containers, adding the syrup and tot of milk from squirt dispensers, mixing them on the Hamilton-Beach DrinkMaster mixers, and laying them out in floor-model freezers until sold. A counter clerk, who could be a boy or girl, would reach into the cabinet, pull out the appropriate milkshake and re-stir it on another mixer to loosen it up.

All of this went on outside one of three windows in front; there was no sit-down dining. Indeed, in those days there wasn't even a restroom for patrons, which made every yard in the surrounding neighborhood vulnerable to the urgent call of nature.

Mike enjoyed his new job and especially the dollar and twenty-five cents an hour he was paid, which sometimes included overtime. You were busy enough that time passed quickly, the people you worked for were pleasant and the entertainment outside the sloping windows was always a plus. Particularly at night, and more than ever on the weekends.

To begin with, this was cruisin' strip numero uno. Hoity-toity Roosevelt high-schoolers showed up in Daddy's day car, cherried Corvette or plush-white-interior convertibles, usually adorned by a "cute" passenger with a beehive 'do. Less-fortunate types from nearby Lincoln High were there, too, but in their pickups, primered Chevys, or Volkswagen Beetle or two. Occasionally, one might spy a souped-up hotrod and its show-off driver, usually surrounded by an envious crowd of straw-slurping Lookie-Lous, at one corner of the lot.

Football nights were crazy, above all if the Teddies and Lynx were playing, because it might mean a rumble. But that happened rarely. Occasionally there'd be a good fight in the parking lot. More often than not it was between individuals battling over a girl or an insult. But a good one could empty out the cars and become a smoker-sized spectator sport until the cops arrived, usually within five to ten minutes, from the Wallingford precinct eight short blocks away.

The glassy box that was the drive-in encapsulated the workers, dressed in white shirts and pants or skirts and wearing paper "soda jerk" caps, and protected them from the outside. Mike's job, as with the rest, was to prepare and serve food, not break up fights. And unless the manager himself called the police, nothing much was done.

In the summer, from opening at 11 A.M. until closing at 2 A.M., a steady-yet-unorganized parade of young women with abbreviated clothing kept Mike and the other male workers observing. Cute boys, with their dipsy-doodle haircuts that were all the rage at the time, kept the females titillated.

In the wintertime, things could get a little drifty, and not so much was worth caring about in the parking lot. Except the occasionally steamed-up car off at one of the side parking stalls. That got Mike's attention, and it often collected a crowd.

Mike worked part-time at Dick's on Forty-fifth Street for two years, until he graduated from high school and—yes, finally!—in the spring acquired his own car, a '55 Studebaker Commander. Before he actually got it, however, he had an incident that involved a car belonging to another Dick's employee named Arlene.

Arlene was a sophomore at Seattle Pacific University and, like Mike, a part-timer at the Wallingford store, and one of the best hand-scoopers the milkshake department ever had. The two found themselves often on the same shift and got to be chummy as workmates. One night before graduation, Mike needed wheels to take his girlfriend Dolly to the movies, and since the Studie wasn't quite his, he asked Arlene if she would loan him her Mercury for the evening, promising to have it back to her by closing. She agreed.

The date was spectacular, and Mike drove like a champ, having only recently received his certificate from the Kirshner Driving School on Roosevelt. But on the way back to Dick's, along Sand Point Way, something went bump—more like *kersplat*, with a grinding follow-up—and he knew he was in deep doo. Barely able to drive, with a temporary license and no adult with him, he found himself guiding the broken car to the curb at 1:10 in the morning. He called Arlene, who wasn't thrilled by the news but was remarkably understanding, and told her where he was. She had a tow truck pick up the car, with a chagrined Mike, and bring them back to Dick's. It turned out a bolt had sheared off and the A frame fell onto the pavement. It would've happened at that time no matter who was driving.

No one knew that Mike was driving when the accident occurred, and he wasn't held responsible, but it did put a little unintended strain on the relationship between workmates.

Soon after Mike got his car, he gunned it up a hill and directly into the side of a mother driving her daughter along Thirty-fifth Avenue Northeast. No one was injured.

It also just happened to be the end of Mike's career at Dick's

Drive-in, but for no particular reason except that it was time to move on, take a new turn and march to a different drummer—namely that of his improving garage band, The Spades. One hell of a summer was brewing, one that would make even a Friday night at the venerable restaurant pale in comparison.

Suffice to say, Dick's continued on as the place to go and be seen, even to this day. The prices are up, more variety in the menu, the competition greater, even among the Dick's chain itself, since new stores were built over time, even as late as 2011.

But one thing never changes, and probably never will, and that is that Dick's is the place where TASTE is the difference, and don't let anyone tell you differently.

# HAIL! HAIL! ROCK 'N' ROLL!

Brother Roger got his groupie on late in life, enjoying the worship of rock 'n' roll heroes when most of them had become cancer-ridden, feeble and gray but still capable of performing almost as well as in the olden days. No spring chicken himself, Roger could brag that within just a couple of months, he'd met and got autographs from Little Anthony of the Imperials, Booker T. Jones and Dick Dale, not to mention local icons like the late Kent Morrill of the Fabulous Wailers and Don Wilson of The Rock and Roll Hall of Fame Ventures.

One could say all this resulted from events that occurred many decades earlier, at a time when the impressionable younger man found himself in the midst of the local "garage band" scene that would place Seattle on the map regionally, nationally and to some degree internationally back in the early Sixties. He couldn't find middle C on a piano, but he sure loved instrumentalists from Johnny and the Hurricanes to Link Wray and Duane Eddy and maintained a prodigious collection of 45s showcasing their work.

As it turned out, his pal Mike once played electric piano ("keyboardist" was a term that would come later) with a purely white group ironically calling itself The Spades. It comprised two members of a youth cowboy band with television experience, Pat and Doug, as well as an exceptional drummer named Vern, Mike and Roger's mutual friend Jules on bass and an off-and-on collection of saxophonists, some good and some not, who filled out the wailing sound prevalent among rock combos at the time. Patrick, for a grease-monkey's love of a rusty old Model T he inherited from an uncle, could never quite make it to rehearsal, so he dropped out, but the others held in there and made a fair showing at many Saturday-night high school dances.

Mike just happened to have access to a seldom-used soundproof radio studio in the basement of KOMO on Fourth and Denny, owing to the fact his father had an office in the building, and every Saturday morning the band members would gather on the step-up stage and rock and roll for hours without interference. Anyone who wished could come and watch from the floor, just as free-ticket holders had done years before the advent of television when radio dramas and musical talent shows were performed on the very same riser. One regular was Mike's neighbor, Tom, who happened also to have a rare reel-to-reel Ampex tape recorder, and a number of weekend sessions were recorded, as were some of the dances themselves a little later.

Mike, Jules, Rick, Doug and Vern the drummer—collectively The Spades—rock 'n' roll at a Bellevue High School gig in 1962. The Seattle-Tacoma area was fertile ground for garage bands at all stages of development. Outfitted by the likes of Fender, Wurlitzer and Ludwig, dozens (perhaps hundreds) of them aspired to duplicate the fame and fortune of the trendsetting Wailers ("Tall Cool One"), Ventures ("Walk, Don't Run") and Frantics ("Werewolf"). (M. Barrett Collection)

In the spring of 1962, when Seattle was in thrall of celebrating its Century 21 Exposition—a fully sanctioned World's Fair—someone came up with the brilliant idea of staging a Battle of the Bands.

They invited, appropriately, twenty-one garage groups to perform separately at the Moore Theatre downtown, and no legitimate ensemble searching for gigs would be turned away. The competition was intense, with no-name talent from all over the region fighting for notice and approval since none to date had ever cut a real record—at least one accepted as playable by a local radio station. And such class names they were: The Penguins, Thundermen, Regents ... and, yes, The Spades, which luckily placed second to the new Continentals with renewed bragging rights and an enthusiastic new marketing scheme.

Competition was particularly keen in getting gigs in those days, in part because of the large number of cheap-yet-adequate garage groups in the area—some say as many as two hundred fifty. The Spades got their share of jobs at Roosevelt and Queen Anne, because most of the band members were from those high schools. Newer institutions in the north end—Ingraham and Nathan Hale, to name a couple—also booked The Spades for dances. But it was more difficult to break into the "ethnic" schools in the south end of town—until two things happened.

The first was the discovery of a young freshman named Kathy, who looked and sang just like Brenda Lee. She attended Rainer Beach and helped get the band a pair of Saturday-night dances, just by being there to belt out Little Miss Dynamite's "Yessiree" and "I'm Sorry."

The other was Cleveland, one of Seattle's three primarily minority-majority high schools before busing.

Mike, as the designated leader, had made contact with the dance chair named Marilyn Woo and set up an audition using Tom's studio-recorded reel-to-reel tape. It would be a snap, he thought, convincing this Chinese-American teenager to hire his group.

But when he arrived, Marilyn shepherded him into a small meeting room wherein sat a contingent of dance committee members numbering not one, not two, but *eight* African-American kids, all slouched in hard-backed chairs with obvious "prove-yourself" attitude engraved on their faces. Of course Mike realized the ramification of his combo's name but never figured there'd be a problem—until that moment. How do you sell an ensemble called

The Spades to a bunch of black kids in a predominately minority high school?

Very carefully.

Sheepishly, the band leader began by introducing himself, followed by a brief pitch (which contained not a lick about race relations) to the attentive crowd. Then he played two of the rock combo's best songs for them to hear. No questions were asked; no eyes were rolled.

Ah, and yes, The Spades did get the job. The Cleveland dance was a huge success, coming off with no rancor or animosity: just a lot of down and dirty boogying. Our story probably would not have unfolded this way just four years later when race riots ripped apart several major cities across the nation.

Brother Roger and a host of other followers of that period rarely missed a concert. Indeed, besides the Saturday-night gigs and the rehearsals at KOMO, there were always the Friday-night visits to the legendary Spanish Castle halfway to Tacoma, or to Parkers Ballroom in the north end, or even to the Lake Hills Roller Rink, of all places, to watch and learn from the local heavies: Dynamics, Frantics, Checkers, Viceroys, Exotics, Bluenotes and, of course, the Wailers. It was as though music had become the imperative, among both musicians and their groupies, and nothing was going to keep them from wallowing in it, or so they thought.

It was about this time The Spades decided to join the American Federation of Musicians Local 76 in Seattle, which allowed them to command higher prices for their gigs. It seemed like a very good move at the time, but it might have come a little too late. They had tried to keep pace with the startling growth of rock 'n' roll in Seattle and elsewhere, but it wasn't easy. It was a primarily instrumental group with few vocals—Mike could do a mean Ray Charles but that was about it—and they were better at pounding out driving drum licks than dancing kicks in tandem on stage. More innovative bands were adapting rhythm-and-blues tunes like "Can't Sit Down" and "Genevieve" into their repertoires, as well as incorporating solo or harmony singing wherever possible. But The Spades couldn't make that transition and began to fall out of favor.

Today, a surprising number of small-time groups from the past continue to play the circuit, but mainly because they once cut a record that, although a flash in the pan, rose high enough on the charts to maintain popularity from generation to generation. Perhaps had The Spades done the same, it would still be playing today, if not as an original group, at least as a name—but then, with *that* name, maybe not.

It's better to know that Doug and Vern and Jules and Mike and Kathy—and Dale and Jeff, the saxes, and Pete, another "keyboardist" who played on occasion—had their two-and-a-half-year fling as garage-band musicians, made a few bucks on weekends to buy beer and cigarettes and experienced the art of performing before, if not adoring, at least receptive fans in the Seattle area, long before Jimi Hendrix, Nirvana or Pearl Jam ever did.

And as for Brother Roger, he still has an old Rock-Ola 450 jukebox carefully preserved in his garage. Every now and then he's drawn there with a beer in hand to play some of the old-timey 45s he's collected over the years and ponder the days of honest-to-god rock 'n' roll.

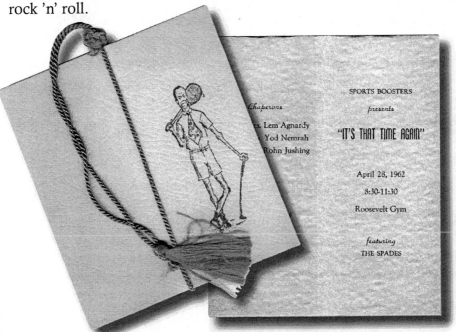

An artifact dating back to one of the dances played by The Spades at Roosevelt High. The program was the handiwork of a dicty dance committee and lampooned the school's clueless tennis coach and boys' health-education teacher, Melvin Dranga, the butt of endless practical (and often tasteless) jokes. While a few slipped through, the faculty confiscated the programs two days before the dance. (R. Miller Collection)

# THE $10,000 FOOTBALL

Boosters and eager city fathers sold the scheme wrapped in tinseled civic pride to a big village that, really, was quite content with the way it was in the Fifties. The only disparaging word was voiced by a small contingent—the vanguard of the "crackpot" Lesser Seattle movement—who chose to boycott the whole shebang during those hemorrhoidal months in 1962. Elitist snobs aside, many more were won over by the gee-whizzery of landing a sanctioned World's Fair set to follow the gala thrown by Brussels in 1960. These were the true blue who, a decade later, would recall the homespun production with warm, fuzzy memories as they cleaned out a drawerful of facsimile Space Needle salt and pepper shakers and tarnished Century 21 trade dollars that had never been redeemed. The rest looked beyond the slick media hype aimed at putting the Queen City on the map, and reckoned what the Big Carnival would be worth in real dollars and cents.

Hucksters everywhere cut through the high-minded talk of community enrichment and set about calculating profit margins. The Century 21 Expo rightly looked to be the biggest economic windfall to hit Seattle since the B-17's around-the-clock assembly lines had come into being with the World War II defense effort. The wide-spread expectation of a pending boom washed over the town from lofty heights and was as contagious as preschool pinkeye. Not surprising, considering the makeup of the one hundred sixteen-man and seven-woman Board of Trustees.*

The leadership drew from the cream of the local mid-Twentieth Century business crop. Included on the list of civic luminaries were Joshua Green, Sr. and Henry Broderick (patriarchs of banking and real

---

* However, the thirty-member corporation actively overseeing the fair counted not a single female in its ranks.

estate); hotelier S. W. Thurston and his right hand, Edward Carlson; prominent retailers Leo Weisfield, Joe Gandy and Paul Friedlander; beer and baseball baron Emil Sick; media moguls William Blethen and J. Elroy McCaw; alderman and incurable rhapsodist Al Rochester (who first envisioned a World's Fair in Seattle); Norton Clapp (*big money*); and well-connected restaurateur-Vice Chair-board member Victor Rosellini. The august assemblage was fused together by the kind of political stickum that could only be applied by the combined efforts of Seattle's Mayor (Gordon Clinton), the head man in Olympia (Governor Albert Rosellini, Victor's first cousin), and the mightiest flotilla of elected muscle this state has ever shipped off to the other Washington (i.e., powerhouse Senators Warren Magnuson and Henry "Scoop" Jackson, backed by veteran House Members Tom Pelly, Jack Westland and Julia Butler Hansen). The all-star lineup's artful utility man, businessman-state senator-Fair Commissioner-board member Howard Bargreen, enthusiastically added his *giddyap* to the stampede that would cut him a choice piece of the fat hog set to waddle into town on April 21, 1962.

The face of Belltown—not to mention Seattle's self-image—would be transmuted by the World's Fair. Note, in this September 1961 photo, the newly erected concrete monorail supports running up Fifth Avenue. In the distance loom the metal spindleshanks of what in months would become the Space Needle. (Seattle Post-Intelligencer Collection, Museum of History & Industry, Seattle; all rights reserved)

From Sea-Tac to Sno-King, from Points Alki to Sand, Seattle's cash registers stood poised for the onslaught. It was clear from early on that a bevy of warm bodies would be needed to man the NCRs at the Expo site in numbers eventually rivaling the army of extras filling some Cecil B. DeMille film epic. And what an illustrious list of concessionaires to require all those hands! K-D-L Hardware positioned itself to duplicate keys from any area hostelry (although the need for this service was unclear); Carellen Productions stood ready to rent, or sell, *foot* (it was stressed) vibrators; the Bickner Company, wood-burning tools on high, prepped to customize redwood nameplates; while Batt and Conklin tuned up statue-molding machines, presumably for non-nefarious purposes.

And beyond the fair's soon-to-be seething campus? Picture Greater Seattle's hundreds of filling stations, restaurants-cafés-greasy spoons, along with the local lodging industry that ranged from the topflight Olympic Hotel to a host of funky boarding-house accommodations thrown together for the duration. It was foreseen that, should each of these enterprises be forced to hire just three more workers to keep pace with the expected land-office business, the town's limited labor pool would be sucked dry in no time at all. Word made the rounds that the county morgue would have to be searched in order to find all the stiffs necessary to actuate the Washington Athletic Club's vision of the next century.

As 1962 dawned, it had become obvious that the requisite employment resource would have to be expanded. Drastically. And so it was, by mid-April, that virtuous girls from Spokane began to arrive to dispense the tons of caramel corn popped for the occasion; kids from bucolic Skagit Valley made their way to Seattle for the first time to become ticketeers; barkers and roustabouts who normally followed the Northwest's county-fair circuit were recruited to operate rides; Las Vegas dancers hit town to kick, grind and tease for Gracie Hansen and LeRoy Prinz; seasoned East Coast cabbies migrated west to wheel out-of-towners from here to there, the long way, for outrageous fares; and ladies of the night slipped in from as far away as Kansas City to bolster Seattle's carefully cloistered call-girl industry. Every man jack of them was primed to take up where the Alaska-Yukon-Pacific Exposition had left off in 1909.

All signs pointed to a dedicated collaborative citywide effort. The Smith Tower at last had a rival bookend in the conspicuous Space Needle at the other end of town. The storied, but cranky, *Kalakala* was refurbished to effect a fairly consistent schedule on the Bremerton ferry run. At Ye Olde Curiosity Shop, Sylvester the mummy had been outfitted with a new loin cloth. It was rumored that Seattle's beloved amusement park, Playland, had been legislated out of business in order to ensure the success of the fair's overpriced Gayway. And, if any more tangible proof was needed of the city's rambunctious efforts to kick things off, the most dominant unlimited hydroplane of the day, the *Miss Thriftway*, was rechristened *Miss Century 21* for the affair.

Next to the Space Needle, World's Fair visitors were most impressed with the Kalakala ("Flying Bird"). Ornery yet endearing, this wannabe Buck Rogers prop treated out-of-towners to a dash of Seattle's storied, but fading, maritime heritage. Its last day of service, on the Seattle-Bremerton run, was October 2, 1967. (Robert and Nellie Schmidt Collection)

Things were ready to roll.

For years, Roger's dad had part-owned a specialty electrical supply company that earned him a whopping $14,000 per year. That sum, augmented by a modest amount of investment income, meant that his wife could devote her days—like most moms of that era—to homemaking, child steering and inhaling the complete works of Agatha Christie while dabbling in pottery painting. It also accounted for the fact that Roger's dad was able to maintain a savings account totaling a tidy $9,000 at the main branch of Peoples National Bank downtown.

Seattle headquartered three sizable financial institutions in the Sixties, along with the number of piggy-bank-sized lenders like Washington Mutual (long before it had grown huge and fatally piggish). Seattle First National, pioneer Dexter Horton's spawn, was the biggest, followed by National Bank of Commerce and Peoples National. PNB at the time of the fair was still nominally controlled by its founder, Joshua Green, Sr., the larger-than-life Methuselah of the city's business community. Still astonishingly agile in both body and mind, Senior knew where every speck of local dirt was buried clear back to the Great Fire of '89. He was also keenly aware of who his major depositors were, and for how long they had trusted him with their cash. Founding Seattle merchants and lenders of the day kept track of things like that before computers did. Roger's father had banked with Old Josh since the 1930s, and $9,000 was still a lot of money in 1962.

The last months of Roger's high school career flitted by in a haze of partying, movie marathons and cruising the vanishing wilderness of rural King and Snohomish counties. Prim and puckered Roosevelt High was about to be reduced to spotty memory, blessedly replaced by a bigger and better bash down Fifteenth Northeast at the University of Washington. In an ill-advised show of great expectations, the U-Dub had recruited Roger on the weight of spectacular sophomore- and junior-year grades. Admissions hadn't prophesied that the bottom would fall out of his GPA during the Great Bender of 1961-62, and evidently didn't care. June approached with the graduating senior more concerned about the brand of beer he guzzled than what course of studies he would, or could, pursue at the next level. Life in Seattle was a bountiful bowl of cherries in his seventeenth year, promising a glowing—if somewhat ill-defined—future devoid of oversized pits and pitfalls. The draft deferment college attendance granted would keep him out of the Army for the foreseeable future. And after that—who knew?—a couple of years of duty in Germany or Panama, or maybe Korea, might prove to be a gas.

The one thing etched in stone was Roger's resolve to avoid self-employment that coming summer. The brush he had had with free-lance painting the year before was still fodder for recurrent nightmares. But, anyway, the subject of a post-high school job hadn't been broached by the time spring arrived, and Roger took that to mean the four-month sabbatical ahead might come off like a long-awaited hybrid *Gidget-Lost Weekend* sequel. Their teener was the last hope his immediate family had of landing a college degree among them, and ideally his folks had come to embrace the wisdom of letting their second-born enjoy a well-deserved breather before tackling big-league academia. Only the Shadel staff could dare estimate how many cases of Olympia would be needed for him to gear up for the four-year ordeal ahead. Roger guessed the summer's bar bill would dwarf the ninety-five-dollar quarterly tuition his mom and dad were shelling out as a down payment on 1966's sheepskin.

The pipe dream went south on May Day.

"How would you like to do some banking this summer?" his father asked as Tuesday night's dinner was being served.

"Banking?"

"For the World's Fair," his dad elaborated over a steaming plate of creamed chipped beef on sticky white rice.

Roger was initially dazed by both the question and the sight of the main course. "*Banking?*"

"Sure, like you do at school now with the lunch money ..." The famished husband winked at his wife while the corner of a cloth napkin was stuffed between his neck and collar to protect the day's blue knit tie. "... Except you'd be paid."

"For banking."

Roger picked at his dinner as his dad, between mouthfuls, explained. The devil's own idle hands seemed to have clamped themselves over unwilling ears while the whole sorry plot was laid out. Son chose to hear only the disheartening highlights: "Stopped by to bank my paycheck today ... Jim, the assistant manager ... having a hard time keeping up with all the concession money coming in ...

more than anybody thought … it's been awfully hard for Peoples to find the right kind of young men … I told him you had exactly the kind of experience he was looking for … at first, Jim thought you might be a little young … looking for maturity on this crew … you'd have to wear a tie … so it's set up that you'll meet me outside the main branch at three-thirty tomorrow."

Without any of it really sinking in until the next morning, Roger awoke to the horror of having committed to a possible life-style-altering job interview with some bank dork that afternoon. Not that she would ever have vigorously opposed her husband's brainstorm, but his mother's barely contained smile had telegraphed her immediate stamp of approval on the plan. She was endorsing it, Roger felt sure, owing to last summer's anguish at seeing her youngest son return home each night with dirty fingernails and paint chips in his hair. God, the humiliation she must have felt beholding her baby displaying blue-collar proclivities!

Roger berated himself for ever having accepted the sixth-period nickel-dime-counting duties at school during his last semester. The spiel from Mr. Oldstem had made the half-credit busywork duty seem like a launchpad to Pan Am's boardroom. As usual, Roger had another angle in accepting the post: What better perk was there than getting out of school twenty minutes early every day? Now, however, he would have gladly stayed an extra hour in order to avoid this unexpected turn of events.

Banking? For a living? Every fiber in his body was repelled by the thought. The prospect was as revolting as looking forward to working for Boeing in Boeingville.

Roger wore slacks and a mother's freshly ironed white shirt that fateful Wednesday. In spite of a seventy-two-cent overage, he bagged up the daily milk receipts, deposited them at the NBofC branch on Roosevelt Way and blazed his way to town down wide-open Eastlake. By the second pass, a parking spot had cleared out just south of the Blue Mouse Theatre. Roger fed the meter a dime to avoid a dreaded dollar parking ticket, quick-hoofed over to Fourth Avenue and reached the front door of Peoples about a minute before his ever-punctual father would have begun pacing.

The branch had closed promptly at 3:00 P.M., as was s.o.p.

throughout the banking community then, but the armed guard posted inside the locked entrance responded smartly to a rap on the thick glass wrapped in polished brass.

"'Lo, Sir," the bank dick, who bore no resemblance to W.C. Fields, called out as he held the door open for the favored customer.

"Afternoon, Cubby. My boy and I are here to see Jim."

They were directed across a shiny marble floor the size of Rhode Island, footfalls sounding more like horses' hooves than neolyte soles and heels. The acoustics in the mausoleum the dollar had built were amazing, instantly transforming the most muted of sounds into audible echoes. As they walked, Roger's ears were filled with clocks ticking, staplers thumping, rubber stamps pounding, cash drawers opening and closing, adding machines madly tallying behind the long row of tellers' cages sealed shut when the clock had signaled finé for finance at the end of the five-hour slot allocated to the banking needs of the bourgeoisie.

The almost total absence of human voices magnified the cathedral-like ambiance of the place. Looking about nervously, Roger caught sight of Cubby unlocking the front door to another party approaching from a chauffeured luxury car parked at the curb. The grand portal swung wide to admit a stick-thin, three-piece-suited old gent who glided into the great room as if he owned it. At the bottom of the sweeping staircase dominating the north side of the lobby the man encountered a young woman descending to the main floor. At the sight of him, the startled lass nearly dropped the pile of files she carried, then did her best to suppress what, without the load in her arms, might have been an involuntary genuflection. The effort earned her a formal doffing of the Twenties-style skimmer the old boy was wearing. That done, the dexterous elder sidestepped the woman to bound up the stairs, two at a time, for the mezzanine above.

Roger turned to find his father staring, mouth agape, in the direction of the ascension.

"That guy must be important, huh?" the son whispered in keeping with where they were.

"*That* was Joshua Green, Senior, himself." The reverential tone of his father's voice was reminiscent of the segregated gallery's acknowledgement of Atticus Finch's courtroom exit in the movie adaptation of *To Kill a Mockingbird.*

Seattle's titans of finance and industry wouldn't be quite so accessible to the guy off the street after the fair was over. Without knowing that, Roger filed the encounter somewhere in his not-*quite*-disposable memory vault.

A moment later, a fiftyish man sporting egregious upper canines (and only nine strands of hair plastered over his baldness) let the pair into an open office area housing loan officials, paper shufflers and a furiously mildewing support staff. The man, it was easy to deduce, was none other than Jim—or Big Jim, as Roger would know him by summer's end. A tepid handshaking ritual was completed before a mimeographed sheet of paper was thrust at him. Roger was slow to realize that he had been given an application form—the very first of countless to follow in the decades ahead.

"I think Jim wants you to fill that out," the dad prompted. "Did you bring a pen?" he addressed his son's empty shirt pocket. Anticipating the answer, the elder already had his Coastal Sales ballpoint out to hand Roger.

The verbal portion of the interview might as well have been a smoke-blowing contest between fathers saddled with indolent adolescent offspring. In fact, Roger's dad supplied almost all of the quasi-substantive information while son toiled over the questionnaire at a remote corner of Jim's huge, dustless desk. When nudged, Roger weighed in with semiconscious responses: "yes"/nod, he possessed a GPA hovering at around three-point-five (excluding the current semester's projected grades); "yes"/nod, he processed and banked school funds every weekday; "yes"/nod, basic math was a snap for him (fortunately, nothing was asked about his grasp of algebra and calculus); "yes"/nod, as far as he had looked into the future he would be attending the University of Washington in the fall.

Owing to a sparse employment history and few non-familial references worth citing, the written form was rapidly completed. Jim gave the signed and dated sheet approximately fifteen seconds of his valuable time, poked the tip of his thumb with the right canine tooth and then directed a financier's astute gaze at the unwilling applicant.

"Nice handwriting, Roger. When can you start?"

It was the beginning of the end for childhood's two-day weekends.

The long summer of banking was almost as much of a blur as his last year at Roosevelt. So was the last third of that year's spring, which was spent working up to full time at Peoples. Ditto the first couple of weeks of autumn until Roger was finally able to cut all ties with his employer and become a frequently hungover fixture that could be seen trudging the hallowed turf between Frosh Pond and Northeast Forty-fifth.

The days, weeks and, finally, months were quickly reduced to the same nose-to-the-grindstone regimen the previous summer had become—minus the lead paint and aching back. The job found him dressed in coat, tie and pressed pants holding a billfold that, for the first time in his life, seldom contained less than a ten spot. It wasn't a full suit of clothes, yet; rather, non-clashing slacks from Bernie's mated with a dark sports jacket off a hanger at MacDougall's. He learned to knot his two-necktie collection from the Tie Rack not long after his eighteenth birthday in June. The ensemble wouldn't have got him past the doorman at the Athletic Club, but he probably could have passed for a Mormon missionary.

He was introduced to encumbrances like time clocks and confusing time cards on top of the insistence that he be on time, all the time. Time at a bank, after all, was money, he quickly found. But the weight of the added baggage was mitigated somewhat by the king's ransom he was being paid—a dollar-ninety per hour—along with perks like time-and-a-half compensation for weeks exceeding forty hours. And there were plenty of them. Not long after his graduation facilitated going full time at Peoples, Roger began grossing more than a hundred a week on average. It was a princely sum that many of the city's Arts & Sciences grads were unable to command right out of the gate, let alone the well-intentioned who had answered the call to join JFK's Peace Corps.

Life during the summer of Sixty-two might have been a drag for Roger, but he was living it in Fat City.

\* \* \*

Seattleites have long loved their coffee. Well before the kick-start beverage became overpriced, burnt-tasting, stupefyingly marketed and fetishistically fancied, the town's grocery shelves verily burst with displays of Butter-Nut, Chase & Sanborn, Fairmont, Boyd's and several brands one could grind to heart's content. Upscalers could even blend their own beans at the neighborhood A&P store. However, step into virtually any diner, hash house, café or cafeteria from Olympia to Blaine and chances were excellent that an empty cup would be filled from a steaming glass carafe stamped "Bargreen's 100% Columbian."

Howard Bargreen had been a potent force in politics dating back to the distant days when he and Henry M. Jackson were pups.[*] (State) *Senator* Bargreen, as he liked to be known, rose to run northwestern Washington's Democratic machine while managing his family's lucrative coffee and restaurant-supply operations. As an oft-elected member of the state legislature, he became a fixture on the Liquor Control Commission, a member of the Commerce, Manufacturing and Licensing Committee, as well as the Ways and Means Committee (and its Revenue and Taxation Subcommittee). By the standards of any era, Howard Bargreen was a man to be seriously reckoned with far outside of his elective district.

The prospect of Seattle landing a World's Fair sent Bargreen's lofty ambitions into orbit. As planning for C-21 ratcheted up, the well-placed senator began acquiring more hats than Bartholomew Cubbins. If Bargreen fell short of becoming the Expo's most influential player, then, at the very least, he could have been crowned its most ubiquitous. By the time the Bureau of International Expositions got around to endorsing Seattle's game plan in 1960, it was hard not to encounter the senator at virtually every stage of lobbying, blueprinting, marketing and governance of the big show. When it opened on Saturday, April 21, Howard Bargreen counted a lion's share of the food concessions on the fairgrounds as part of his edibles empire: hotdogs to pretzels, soda to gelato, popcorn to potato chips. Needless to say, there was more 100% Colombian poured per square foot for the duration than Howard Schultz and his board would ever

---

[*] Bargreen was outpolled by Jackson in the 1940 primary election that inaugurated Scoop's four-decade-long congressional career.

have dared dream. (Bargreen did, however, leave the beer garden concession in the capable hands of up-and-coming racketeer Frank Colacurcio, Sr.)

Now, to handle that mountain of Seattle-bound loot: sort it, bank it, prepare change kits for seed to get more of it. Joshua Green had everything that was needed to get the job done for the real Mr. Coffee.

If the wind was blowing just so, the razzmatazz of the Gayway was faintly audible on the second floor of the PNB branch at Dexter and Broad streets, five blocks away—which was as close to the World's Fair as Roger allowed himself to get while counting the lucre brought in by Howard Bargreen's concessions. Elvis's on-location visit in early September to film a quickie exploitation movie did nothing to lure the novice banker any closer to the grounds.[*]

Hank acted as head teller for the intrepid band of four who, seven days a week, counted the contents of the dozens of blue deposit bags that made their way to the bank by armored truck every morning before opening. A football letterman and graduate of West Seattle High School, Hank had drifted back to his hometown following a hitch in the Army. He had responded to a *P-I* classified ad seeking temporary bank tellers—"no experience needed"/"may lead to permanent employment." Hank was as laid back as Ballard in those days: unassuming, nonjudgmental and—even in the throes of the occasional titanic hangover—even-tempered ... *provided* the daily books balanced and nobody on his crew took himself too seriously.

"Doc" Bates and Stew, together with two alternating PNB regulars, had launched the unique counting room set-up with Hank. Roger joined in mid-May as weekend relief until becoming a full-timer in early June. At twenty-three, Bates was the senior crew member by a few months: a pre-med student at the UofW who had opted out of spring and summer quarters to earn his way back to fiscal good health. His workmates suspected he had spent himself into a corner buying wardrobes from Littler that shamed the off-the-rack Jacques Pennay-style fashions the rest of them wore to work. Bates was an impeccable dresser down to his dimpled silk ties. He

---

[*] Legend has it that Governor Al Rosellini pitched the original idea for *It Happened at the World's Fair* directly to M-G-M. His fee remains unknown.

was cultured, upwardly mobile and, by far, the best educated of the group. On occasion, an unpalatable dose of this refinement would be imposed on the others (as when tuning in classical KXA for a smidge of Mozart while no one was looking), whereupon the crew responded by addressing him not as *Doc* Bates, but as *Master* for the balance of the day. Astute use of this alternate title was a great class equalizer that long summer.

Stew, sporting a tall haystack of Brylcreemed hair, was a couple of years out of high school, although it was never clear whether he was old enough to vote yet. Or ever would. He drove a lowered 1958 Plymouth Savoy, had two very young children at home he seldom spoke about and thought better of broadcasting the fact that he was an evangelical Christian (or Holy Roller, as such folks were labeled then). He was the most subdued of the group, displaying psychotic tendencies only when his till failed to balance at the end of the day. Roger worked at the desk next to him and never felt entirely at ease being that close.

Jim—*Big* Jim, as Hank was wont to call him—ruled the Denny Regrade counting operation from the main branch downtown. Jim was a rising star at Peoples, as demonstrated the following year when he was elevated to the position of manager at the bustling Dexter and Broad branch. Big Jim visited his handcrafted counting house only twice that frantic summer, preferring to delegate day-to-day supervision to a waning star in the company, Abner "Bub" Dee, whose pleated wool slacks smelled of traces of formaldehyde (according to Doc).

Abner's title and precise job description were subjects of constant debate within his own bailiwick. He generally lurked somewhere down on the first floor, acting as a kind of Handler of Widgets and Annoyances, as when someone had to be called to deal with the inexplicable activation of the bank alarm, or when keys for some reason wouldn't fit their assigned safety deposit boxes. Abner was always available to cope with such snafus. And twice each business day, he would ascend to the second floor to peer around the check-processing department, sample food to be served at the in-house cafeteria and check the big Pitney Bowes postage machine to make note of postage credit still available. In all situations, in every area visited, Abner would address each person he encountered with the repetitive salutation, "How's it goin', Bub?" Young or old, male or female, no matter: "How's it goin', Bub?"

That summer, Big Jim added to Abner's list of routinized duties by assigning him to keep an eye on the counting-room cast. This would prove to be a challenge of the first order for all parties concerned.

Peoples Bank provided a lunchroom on the second floor—and not just a space filled with vinyl-top tables, vending machines and enough space for the sixty or so branch employees to wolf down sacked groceries. No, this was the real McCoy, complete with hair-netted kitchen staff, daily specials and a fixed, if simple, hot-meal menu. At fifty cents a serving, no one living on bank wages was heard complaining. Roger, like most, never bothered to brown-bag it.

The counting operation had been shoehorned into the crowded facility by usurping about a quarter of the lunchroom's total square footage. Security concerns were low priority, as evidenced by the flimsy, folding wood partition that had been installed in April to effect the separation of diners from World's Fair loot. A customized Dutch door, originally introduced to facilitate handout food sales, was now the sole access to Hank's sixteen-foot-by-sixteen-foot hideaway. At first, only the bottom half could be locked, much to the delight of Abner whose surprise visits, early in the game, were highlighted by their monitor thrusting his torso through the breachable top to startle the boys with a snappy "How's it goin', Bubs?" Fine, if everyone was tending to business at one of the four counting stands—not so fine, if the crew, as one, had paused to scope out a hot car, a well-endowed young woman or a drunk flumbling his way to the liquor store across the parking lot below.

Big Jim took exception to the open-upper-half-door policy during his first visit in late May. Petty cash paid for a ninety-nine-cent slip lock from the downtown Ernst Hardware store, and instructions were given to Abner to see to its installation. Abner unhappily, but dutifully, complied and from then on reconciled himself to using the foxy seven-knock signal he devised to keep out yeggs and undesirables, such as himself. Hank took great pleasure in dawdling for up to a minute before responding to the knuckled code, blaming the lapse on the loud clatter of the coin-counting machine, or on the roar of the circulating fan in almost constant use.

The downside to keeping Abner from unexpectedly popping in had been Jim's further insistence that both halves of the door be closed and locked at all times. Adequate air circulation within the south-facing cubbyhole effectively ended with his edict. Any day surpassing fifty degrees outside fueled an oven inside in spite of a row of squat, fold-out windows at the base of the giant panes mounted in the outer wall. To his credit, Abner was able to ferret out a castoff fan in the building's basement where it had been stored since a centralized cooling system began servicing the lobby. Once relied upon to move air over all the main floor, the wind machine's DC-3 prop-sized blades, even on a slow-speed setting, created a realistic typhoon effect inside the cramped processing room.

The PNB gig was the callow young man's solemn introduction to the eight-to-five trip ensnaring solid, tax-paying citizens. And looming large over the brutal tedium was the hellish irony of being able to afford things he had never coveted before, of having the resources at last to cruise the Northwest in style. Yet all of it was dangled in front of his nose without allowing Roger the time to squander a hard-earned shekel. It was the kind of scenario that drove some young men to madness. Others to drink.

By the time he clocked out late each afternoon, long after the downstairs tellers had gone home, stores were closing in that retail Stone Age before 7-11s, Midnight Madness Sales and 10:00 P.M. mallathons. The lack of a life grew to a point where he was even forced to excise routine visits to the Warehouse of Music and Stewart & Sullivan on Lake City Way for updates of the Fabulous 50 Music Survey and KOL's Century-21 Survey of Hits. On the provident side of things, however, he was able to put by a good share of his take-home pay despite record after-work beer consumption during the fair. 1962 was destined to become the year he learned to contend with the on-the-job hangover.

May bowed out with C-21 observing American Waterworks Day, and by the time South Dakota had been honored on the Plaza of States (June 10), Hank had fine-tuned the mechanics of the counting-room operation. After the crew assembled upstairs each morning, he unlocked and began dumping out the mashed contents of two, sometimes three, carpetbag-sized carriers in the middle of the floor. There were never fewer than sixty individual deposit bags for the counters to process, and sometimes nearly double that following advertised promotions like Snipe Regatta Day. Such shifts were especially trying for Roger and the others owing to the awful predictability of what harried NCR jockeys were prone to send their way. Hank was the soul of impartiality when it came to divvying up the deposits in four separate piles. Sticky or curiously stained zip-up pokes were always evenly distributed. Their contents were a crapshoot. Sometimes the fattest turned out to be the best-ordered and accurately balanced, while an innocuous-looking thin packet could conceal chaos and no identifying deposit slip. The fate of many of Hank's scrupulously prepared hundred-and-thirty-dollar change kits never failed to surprise, even stun, the greenhorn bankers who untangled the returning shambles the next day.

The cashier's assigned number, usually appearing at the top of each enclosed (it was to be hoped) deposit slip, instantly foretold the condition of the bag's innards. Number Four's infamous trademark was, characteristically, small doughnut pieces compressed between the bills and scattered among the coins. Occasionally caramel corn was substituted, possibly for variety. The mixture of cash and clinging compost worked to prohibit use of the bank's state-of-the-art coin and bill counters for verification of often disputed totals and breakdowns. Number Twenty-one's daily masterpieces looked, upon opening, as if a small explosive charge had been detonated in transit. Number Thirty-eight's bags tended to be unlocked and often included handwritten apologies scrawled on scraps of paper with oddments like bus tokens paperclipped to them. All-time honors, however, naturally went to Cashier Sixty-nine. In eleven attempts during two weeks in July, the unidentified he or she never once managed to deliver an accurate deposit record. The last submission, dated July 20th (designated New Jersey Day at the fair), included a mustard-stained paper napkin inscribed with the message, "FUCK THIS SHIT," along with a nearly fourteen-dollar shortage for good measure.

It required only a few days on the job for the visceral luster of money to be irrevocably tarnished. Roger's reaction wasn't due merely to the muffled nausea that accompanied plucking bits of used Kleenex out of the incoming rat's nests, or the qualms they all had about handling inexplicably wet currency occasionally coated with cotton-candy residue. An especially virulent taint seemed to permeate each of the hundreds, even thousands of bills uncurled, sorted and tallied each day. Their hands became soiled by the grubby paper after processing only a bag or two. On break or at lunch, the crew would dash for the second-floor men's room, not to claim-jump the single urinal, but to crowd around the sink—before peeing—to rid hands and fingers of counter's stickum and the accumulated crud sloughed off by dirty money incoming from all four corners of the earth.

Stew was the least fazed by touching filthy lucre. But, then, Stew was the closest thing to a numismatist there was in the counting room. Not that he was a collector by any stretch of the imagination. He did, however, possess an extraordinary eye for rare and semiprecious coins and bills. Because, in addition to the extraneous flotsam each deposit bag held in the way of gum wrappers and sucked-on Life Savers, each one of the them also had the potential for surrendering a money buff's mother lode. His was quite a different way of looking at legal tender.

In no time at all, Stew had inspired Hank and Roger to begin setting aside the most apparent of above-face-value coins, 1943 zinc-coated pennies. A downtown dealer he frequented paid two cents apiece for them, with a full roll averaging good or better condition going for a buck-and-a-quarter. World War II part-silver nickels, easily spotted because of the big mint mark on the tails side, went for up to fifteen cents. Indian-head pennies and so-called standing-Liberty quarters, while not as common as the others, were very visible and well worth setting aside.

Doc Bates ignored the salvaging sideline until the week after the International Barbershop Quartet Song Fest had wowed fairgoers on July 8th. First, Stew noticed a plain 1928 silver dollar in fine condition that he unloaded for seventy-five bucks. Two days later, Hank sold a 1921 D half-dollar for ninety times face value just as Roger let it drop that he was averaging twenty dollars in profits each week selling his finds to an eager coin-shop owner located on Roosevelt Way. Come American-Norway Day, Doc spied a good-to-fine HAWAII commemorative twenty in among the pretzel crumbs, followed by the discovery of a misprinted five-dollar bill worth four times par to the dealer Hank was doing business with. Shortly after that, Doc began showing up at work with the new fall line of Arrow double-stitched shirts.

Every morning the crew filled swap cups with set amounts of personal coin and currency. As they processed the day-old deposits, worthwhile finds were put aside and their face value replaced from the exchange funds to keep the count honest. Each stand-up desk drawer held its own kind of Gideon Bible, a dog-eared copy of some expert's "official" coin and paper money price guide answering all but the most esoteric questions about American cash. Not that there was ever enough time to examine every incoming centime (actually, two French coins had been included in Number Sixty-nine's memorable swan-song deposit).

Fair attendance was of critical importance to their activity, both on behalf of the bank and their own personal endeavors. If daily turnstile totals topped sixty thousand, Hank and his quick-fingered troopers were hard-pressed to complete the count, balance and lock up the receipts in nine hours. However, when attendance hovered around fifty thousand, or slipped below that mark, the boys could almost always rely on ample time to carefully sort, grade and even debate market value of any desirable monetary unit that came their way. Each morning, Hank helped set the bar by bringing a copy of the *Post-Intelligencer*'s Sunrise Edition on whose front page was printed the previous day's crowd total.*

The fair turned a profit in spite of itself. Patrons stunned by a visit to the cheesy Spacearium were able to regain composure at the Everett DuPen Fountain, which offered communion with "three abstract bronze sculptures depicting the evolution of life from a single cell to man and ... of sea gulls and flowing seaweed." In the Friendship Mall, the Christian Witness Pavilion ordained, for the

---

* The grand total attendance figure for the six-month affair was 9,609,969, or about 53,000 paid admissions per day. Gates ranged from a low of 18,821 on May 1 to a spike of 128,721 on October 20, the day before the fair closed.

spiritually bankrupt, that the only hope open to a world living with the cobalt bomb lay in embracing The Creator. Nearby, the less-troubled could enrich famished intellects at the Nalley's Pavilion by taking in a pickle-making documentary, or by searching out the Carnation Company's animated mechanical cow in the Hall of Industry.

Further to the subject of appetites, physical sustenance was, of course, always just steps away from the centrally located Food Circus. If a survivor found himself hungry following fifteen feet of heart-pounding levitation on the Bubbleator at the Washington State Coliseum, a festal board awaited that included delicacies like Four Winds Po-Boys, Edmar Protein Shakes, Stewart In-Fra-Reds and those stick-to-the-palate morsels from Cashmere, Aplets and Cotlets (well-licked, the latter provided especially effective, if disgusting, ammunition when dropped on the heads of the unwary strolling forty feet below the Skyride—i.e., those thinly disguised bomber buckets that floated, nonstop, above the grounds from the Gayway to the International Mall).

Forecasting technology in the New Millennium was a popular theme. At the General Motors exhibit, for example, one could inspect the car that visionary transportation engineers swore the country would be rodding around in when the century turned. The Firebird III, sans steering wheel, was an automatically guided sure thing featuring more fins than a guided missile. There was no mention of its anticipated mileage, nor any best-guess estimates about the value of GM stock come 2009.

Highbrow entertainment at the Big Carnival did no favors for anyone's bottom line. Upon occasion, C-21 programmers forgot that a healthy dose of culture for most early Sixties' Seattleites meant attending a one-night stand by Andy Williams, or swatting mosquitoes on Green Lake while taking in a jolly session of the Aqua Follies. Poor gates for on-site events spelled diminished sales at Bargreen's concessions, and vastly reduced chances of finding a Barber dime or a gold certificate among the bankables. A week-long presentation of *Waiting for Godot* and the appearance of the Old Vic players for a five-day engagement didn't hold a flickering candle to the allure of a live telecast of *The Ed Sullivan Show* from the fair, or the excitement generated by the Roy Rogers and Dale Evans extravaganza that slipped over into July at the Stadium.

It was either bring on the circus or close up shop early at the Seattle World's Fair.

When it was slow, monotony sometimes supplanted avarice. Idle hands developed bad habits that, among other things, led to deteriorating air quality in the counting room. Small wonder. Because a pack was only thirty cents out of the lunchroom vending machine, a consumer really couldn't afford not to indulge in the favorite vice of one out of two Americans. Roger, who had avoided smoking cigarettes all through high school, finally bought his first pack of butts, Chesterfield Kings, as the summer stumbled into August. Unaware then that the same brand of straights had contributed to the death of fifty-seven-year-old Humphrey Bogart in 1957, Roger was inhaling with the best of them by the end of the month. (Two years later, the federal government would mandate a printed warning to smokers from the Surgeon General advising the hazards of feeding the nic habit.)

Hank knew inertia when he saw it. Like most MBAless managers of the day, he took direct steps to counteract its deleterious effect on his charges. His remedy was simplistic as it was dynamic, and out-and-out revolutionary in the sense that it flew in the face of every accepted banking custom: Hank brought a radio to work. Wisely, he put himself in charge of supervising use of the two-band Emerson (which was stashed behind a drawn drape covering part of the inside window ledge). The tuner never strayed from the AM band, in spite of occasional requests to try out a couple of fledgling FM signals. Nor did the dial exceed the range of fifty ticks separating 950 and 1000 kilocycles.

When the Emerson was on, KJR ruled, as it did most everywhere in Seattle then, addressing prickly questions of the time like the odds of the Belmonts ever again topping the charts without Dion, or how many plays would be necessary to make one physically ill listening to Tony Bennett croon "I left my heart in San Francisco." Hank's boredom-busting radio became as vital to the crew's well-being as the electric fan in spite of the teenybopper dreck infecting the pop charts that summer—foremost among the dreadful: Dickie Lee's "Patches," Jimmy Clanton's "Venus in Blue Jeans" and Shelley

Fabares' endlessly overdubbed "Johnny Angel" (which Roger retitled "Johnny Jerk-off," with appropriately altered lyrics).

The monophonic speaker was never conspicuously loud Monday through Friday, even given the temptation to goose the volume whenever "Green Onions," Tommy Roe's "Sheila" or the breakout "Surfin' Safari" were spun. Saturdays and Sundays, however, when the big building was as dead quiet as the offices of Scrooge & Marley, the radio was unmuffled for Del Shannon, The Crystals, Dave "Baby" Cortez and, especially, for Hank's personal theme song and anthem, Freddy Cannon's "Palisades Park." The head teller never failed to sing along with the line, "We ate and ate at the hotdog stand," immortal words to which he ascribed heavy Freudian meaning that brought to mind past back-seat glories each time he heard the stompin' tune.

No fan of pop music, Doc Bates was mortified when a family vocal trio, the Browns, released their version of the ancient Sinatra hit, "The Old Master Painter." Taking liberties with the noun in the title, the office chorale delighted in serenading him long after the DJ had gone to commercial. Fortunately for the medic-to-be, the tune failed to crack thirty on the KJR chart and was aired only sparingly. Connie Francis teased them all with the "V-A-C-A-T-I-O-N" that would never be until the fair closed in October, while Carole King's first hit, "It Might as Well Rain Until September," more than once dampened the mood in the room. Still, the Establishment-defying radio kept young fingers flying, absenteeism at zero and ending tallies right on the button.

The only time the dial setting changed under Hank's watch was right after weekday lunches. For years before and after C-21, KOMO broadcast a network-wide quasi-news feature that beamed across Puget Sound country in various time slots. The staccato-voiced reporter regaled a devoted audience with offbeat, but guaranteed, twenty-four-carat accounts of the less apparent side of current events, noteworthy anomalies and history revisited with a novel slant. There were stories uncovering what else U.S. brass considered doing with the atomic bomb at the close of World War II; details of the unusual bond between celebrated author Sir Arthur Conan Doyle and magician Harry Houdini; a reading of the fan letter bank robber and public enemy John Dillinger wrote Henry Ford, Sr.; light cast on how hubris accounted for the *Titanic* disaster—in all, tons of fascinating frippery that totally captivated Hank. The stale world of banking—the planet Earth, for that matter—ceased to exist until Paul Harvey dismissed his steadfast listener with the signature sign-off, "Goood *daaay!*" By summer's end, the entire crew was hooked.

Although universally viewed as being far from the brightest penny in the roll, Abner did sense that there were violations of banking decorum, not to mention federal law, ongoing behind the locked Dutch door. Abner's undersized imagination, however, simply wouldn't allow him to grasp the scope and frequency of the counting crew's transgressions. The softly playing radio and laughter from within were barely countenanced. On the other hand, the numismatic sideline would have caused a noisy scandal, if it had been detected. The youthful staff's salty language and ribald humor flew in the face of industry-wide stodginess. Joshua Sr. would have been felled by apoplexy had he ever got wind of the crew's habitual disregard for PNB's dress code. After lunch and Paul Harvey, the lads typically ditched both coats and ties, and the day's stretch run often found them down to T-shirts in the smoky, wind-whipped heat. The only meaning *etiquette* had for the bad boys of banking was that the word doubled for the name of the record label owned by Tacoma's Wailers.

More than anything in the world, Hank wanted to play football. He had been a three-year letterman for the West Seattle Indians handling dissimilar duties as lineman and sometimes punter for his team. The opportunity to indulge his passion while serving in the Army further whetted his appetite for the game. Grades, however, kept him out of the University of Washington and Jim Owens' wildly successful gridiron program. For a time he considered auditioning for Don Sprinkle's Ramblers semi-pro team. But experience and observation ultimately led Hank to a dispiriting epiphany: Although rock hard and well conditioned, he was simply too small to effectively compete with starting linemen who had five inches and forty pounds on him. Yet his fervor was sustained by a city that was still sky high on rose fumes following the Huskies' stunning upset wins in

Pasadena in 1960 and '61 (never mind the past season's 5-4-1 Big Six second-place comedown). Though he never spoke about it, deep down Hank believed he could punt a football better than anybody wearing a purple-and-gold jersey. That summer he spent more time putting his private claim to the test with former Indians' teammates than he did at the Jigsaw Tavern across the street from the Admiral Theatre.

The upcoming football season began to compete for Seattle's infatuation with the four-month fuss at the foot of the Space Needle. As the 1962 opener with Purdue neared, the bulk of counting-room chitchat likewise began to focus on Washington's prospects for the highly anticipated campaign. Roger was especially pumped. Since 1958, he had eagerly watched the antics of the student section from seats shared with his dad across the field in the Iron Monster. Now, as an incoming freshman (temporarily in good standing), he would at least be able to join in the aerial garbage fights, help pass hapless student bodies around the roiling stands, concoct ingenious ways of sneaking forbidden alcohol into the games—Great Glory, could a university education offer anything better?

Every chance he got, Stew showed off a garish husky dog key ring his wife had given to him after some communion or other in June. Even Doc, far from being the rah-rah type, was corrupted by football fever. By late August, young Dr. Kildare was angling for fifty-yard-line seats on the Tyee Club side in hopes of avoiding Roger's kindred riffraff in the student section. And Hank? Day after day he patiently bided his time, awaiting the Big Play.

They had balanced out by 3:00 P.M. on a fly-droning Wednesday not long after the Folkloric Ballet of Mexico allegroed out of town in early September. Efforts to kill a little time before punching out produced a broom none of them had seen in weeks, a feather duster nobody even knew about and a small can of Energine with just enough left in it to clean off the accumulated grime coating the tops of their work stations. Shortly after wiping down the bill counter that never worked—and, perhaps, under the influence of the raw solvent fumes wafting over his corner—Hank began offhandedly fiddling with the contents of his immaculately arranged, vault-bound cash cart.

When Roger looked up from reading a flyer promoting the Uday Shankar Dancers scheduled in October, he found the head teller standing by the door playing one-handed catch with a rubber-banded brick of currency. There was an odd cast to his eyes, he noticed at once, not unlike their appearance early Sunday mornings when, smelling like Four Roses, Hank let them into the deserted building. Yet this look was somewhat different. More focused. Almost demented.

Ray Charles had barely got into "You Don't Know Me" behind the drape when Doc observed their leader's rigid stance altered only by the hypnotic juggling of five hundred bound bills. Twenties, Doc was almost sure. Ten thousand dollars worth. Stew jumped to attention when Hank cleared his throat authoritatively, a sign that frequently caused the pious young man to mentally cross himself.

"Here's the deal," Hank told them when they had all turned to face him. The bundle was now clamped firmly in a big, strong right hand. His audience tuned out Ray to listen. "The Huskies are backed up on their own eight-yard line," *the* man began explaining. "It's third and fourteen and the Boilermakers are gonna rush everybody in town because Monroe and Coffee are out—injured. Only Mitchell is back to block for Siler."

"Jesus," Roger whispered at the gravity of the situation.

Stew was wheezing tension barely a foot away.

"Here's what we do."

Everyone froze.

"Stew, you have kids—you be the center." Hank slung the $10,000 football at the teller's solar plexus. Three years of Pop Warner League drills came back to Stew during the short flight, and the center-elect snagged the paper brick in rat-trap mitts. "Doc, Roger—you're blocking ends split, opposite sides, as far off Stew as you can get. On a three-count—hut, hut, *HUT!*—drop back two steps, then take out Purdue's rushing ends. Centerman, hike on the same count, block their interior line—and fall on your face."

Roger tore off the jacket he had just put on and slung it over the back of his high chair in such a way that Doc wouldn't be able to see the brand label stitched to its lining. Doc opted to guard the left side, leaving Roger to flank Stew four feet to the right. The first "hut" clued the pair of outside linemen to assume the three-point stance. The second brought Hank up from a gargoyle-like crouch for a false show of offensive intent that failed to draw the Boilermakers offside. One beat later, PNB's QB barked the command to center the ball. Stew hiked the bundle of bucks as skillfully as a ten-dollar Voit. Hank, eight feet behind him, took the deep snap and pretended to bobble it to buy seconds while Stew took cheap shots at phantom knees. Only after the center had prostrated himself on the gray and white linoleum did it become clear what play Coach Owens had sent in from the sidelines. Doc and Roger hindered chalkboard tacklers before glancing back to find Hank stepping forward to get off an astonishing third-down punt.

Part Nureyev, part Bob Schloredt—an unlikely partnering bedecked in factory-cut gabardine—the point of Hank's scuffed right Buster Brown swept up to meet the ersatz football with Annie Oakley accuracy. The timing, contact and follow-through combined to make Hank's punt a thing of true beauty. The trouble was, the only material opponent in the room—the great circulating fan—hadn't been taken into account by the blocking scheme. The thing loomed up, just beyond the line of scrimmage, like six-foot-seven Oakland Raider, née Husky, Ben Davidson, who was able to swat clouds out of the sky while standing on the flats of his feet. The route of the projectile simply didn't have sufficient lift built in to allow it to clear the swirling beast.

Two of the five interior paper straps, along with one of the half-inch rubber bands binding the packets, had already ruptured following the impact with the punter's shoe. When the fracturing bale of cash collided with the metal cage surrounding the wicked blades, it struck with enough force to mimic the effect of a pressurized feather pillow exploding in space. The last paper straps and big rubber bands called it quits at very close to the same millisecond and resulted in five hundred twenty-dollar bills taking to the stormy air like billowing goose down. And in the midst of the blinding greenback blizzard was heard a sound at the Dutch door as chilling as anything recorded in the Old Testament:

knock-knock-knock-knock-knock ... *knock-knock*

Hank, through a quarter-inch gap in the door, informed an inquisitive Abner Dee that he was interrupting a vitally important staff meeting. Abner retaliated by telling Hank that meetings of the counting-room crew couldn't be sanctioned on the bank's time because the counting-room crew wasn't classified as regular staff. While Stew, Doc and Roger frantically scooped up errant bills behind him, Hank rebutted that, owing to the fact that the counting room was half-staffed, it was entitled to ad hoc merit reviews. Abner had no idea what *ad hoc* meant, nor how seriously to take a veiled threat of citing the Geneva Convention. In the end, he left in a huff, promising the head teller he would return with an official ruling from Big Jim.

Fifteen minutes passed before the lathered agent returned with a cease and desist order from the head office. During that time, the lads reduced the $10,000 shortage on the vault cart to twenty dollars, but were forced to temporarily call off the search for the missing bill when Abner was admitted to lay down the law. His rant was cut short when Hank broke in to confess that Abner's first visit had interrupted a long overdue, soup-to-nuts cleaning of the room they had hoped to surprise their Big Bub with. Abner left with tears in his eyes after a cursory inspection, whereupon Hank and his lieges tore the place apart again.

The missing bill was never found. They counted the reassembled stack of twenties ten times over, moved every stick of furniture to the center of the room to snoop in dusty recesses, and even dispatched Roger to wander around the parking lot as inconspicuously as possible in the vain hope the ghostly green had been sucked out one of the barely cracked windows. No dice.

At last giving in to futility, the crew wound up passing the hat to cover the shortage. Hank guaranteed repayment to all and sent Doc next door to see Agnes, lunchroom cashier and hot-tray diva, about converting the donated bills and sundry change. Ironically, the twenty he returned with was a 1928 Woods-Mellon series gold certificate, in very fine condition. Without hesitation, however, it was consigned to the light packet and banded along with ninety-nine others. Hank rolled the cash cart to the vault at 5:40. He and his team clocked out six minutes later with almost an hour of overtime to show for the blown play.

The Huskies opened the season at home on September 22 with what turned out to be a yawner. They tied Purdue, seven-up, before a fidgety crowd of 56,000 that came for blood, but had to settle for sweat. Neither team resorted to a third-down punt.

Roger left the bank a little more than three weeks after the misadventure to begin an undistinguished five-year stand at the UofW. A rare highlight was never missing a home football game where, true to form, Doc Bates was not to be found in the seething student section. Nor did Hank's name ever appear in the game programs Roger read faithfully. The freshman and retired banker promptly withdrew all the funds from his employee checking account at PNB and deposited them in the more convenient University Village branch of NBofC. Not a cent of Roger's savings remained by the following February.

A quarter of a century later, Peoples National Bank was absorbed by Portland-based U.S. Bank. By then, the Bubbleator was serving as a greenhouse in Redondo. And Seattle, now with an unquenchable thirst to make a name for itself on some kind of list or other, wasn't anything like the Seattle before the Big Show.

Not quite an amusement park ride, nor even very amusing, the Bubbleator and its ability to leaven crowds at the Washington State Coliseum were about as pulse-pounding as riding the elevators at Rhodes department store—and a lot slower. Apparently fairgoers were easily enthralled, for it was among the Expo's most popular attractions. (Courtesy of Museum of History & Industry, Seattle; all rights reserved)

# ACKNOWLEDGEMENTS

The authors owe a great debt and many thanks to Jim Engelhardt (classmate and sometimes accomplice back when) for cover design and book layout; likewise, to the staff at the downtown branch of the Seattle Public Library and, in particular, to Bo Kinney who introduced us to the perceptive work of photographer Werner Lenggenhager; to Carolyn Marr of the Museum of History and Industry for help tracking Seattle's photo footprint mid-century; Dave Williams of the Hydroplane & Raceboat Museum in Kent; Lindsey McGuirk of Village Books in Bellingham for publishing guidance and printing midwifery; for the assistance of numerous and patient staffers manning University of Washington Special Collections and the news file department; to the great, late Emmett Watson (founder of Lesser Seattle) for decades spent monitoring the Queen City's pulse and for the many insights he left behind; to those members of AU who lived to tell about it; and, of course, to the Old Town that inspired this work by providing the best setting for growing up any kid ever had.